lynn, alex and dave

Collier's Rules for DESKTOP DESIGN AND TYPOGRAPHY

Characters

Typefaces and Fonts

Words and lines

Punctuation

Paragraphs

Illustrations and graphics

Page layout

Printing and Binding

Colour

cument handling

HyperMedia

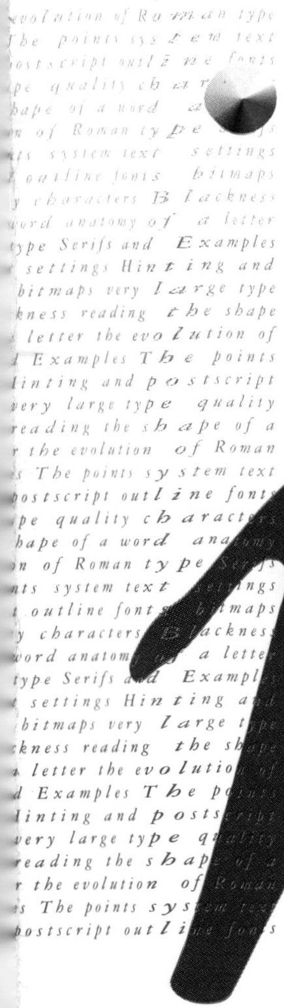

David Collier · DeCode Design

Addison-Wesley Publishing Company
Wokingham, England · Reading, Massachusetts · Menlo Park, California · New York
Don Mills, Ontario · Amsterdam · Bonn · Sydney · Singapore · Tokyo
Madrid · San Juan · Milan · Paris · Mexico City · Seoul · Taipei

Cover designed by Paul Khera and
printed by The Riverside Printing Co. (Reading) Ltd.

Typeset in 8 and 9 point New Baskerville by DeCode Design, W1.

Imageset by Midford Typesetting, W1 and Thorndale Benedict, WC1.

Printed and bound in Great Britain by The Bath Press, Avon.

First printed 1990. Reprinted in 1991.

Written and Art Directed by David Collier.

Designed and Illustrated by Lynn Clark and Alex Gollner.

Edited by Carol Atack of *MacUser* magazine, London.

Copy edited by Alison Ritchie.

Hypertext chapter written by Tim Carrigan of *Multimedia* magazine, London.

Additional information for colour chapter from Paul Holmes of Computers Unlimited, almost London (081).

Additional information for designing fonts from Vince Whitlock of the Letraset Type Directorate, London.

Intelligent PostScript fonts by Nigel Yeoh.

Index compiled by Peter Banks.

Contributions gratefully received (in alphabetical order) from Roger Black, Steven Coates at Blueprint, Len Cheeseman at CDP, Simon Esterson at Esterson Lackersteen, Andreas Harding, Paul Khera, Adam Levene at Cartlidge Levene, Nico Macdonald at Spy, Will Meister the MacMan and Eric Spiekermann at Meta Design.

Thanks to: Amanda Callaghan, Patrick Stewart, Sylvia, John and David Lynch.

Dedicated to Nellie McQueen for opening my eyes: A^x.

Joy to all DeCode associates and digital designers. FutureMedia is yours.

British Library Cataloguing-in-Publication Data
Collier, David *1966-*
Collier's rules for desktop design and typography.
1. Desktop publishing
I. Title
070.50285416

ISBN 0–201–54416–4

Library of Congress Cataloging-in-Publication Data
Collier, David, 1966-
Collier's rules for desktop design and typography / David Collier.
p. cm.
Includes index.
ISBN 0-201-54416-4
1. Desktop publishing—Style manuals. 2. Printing, Practical–Layout—Data-processing. I. Title II. Title: Rules for desktop design and typography.
Z286.D47C65 1991
686.2'2544—dc20 90-46138
CIP

GRAPHIC design is a pretty new profession, the last in a series of job descriptions resulting from the dividing of labour in the publishing trade, which has now become part of what is no longer referred to as a trade: the Graphic Arts Industry.

Gütenberg designed his own type, engraved it, cast it in lead, composed it, made his own ink, printed the books and bound them. As the job got more complicated, different people took on some of the more specialised jobs: there would be engravers, typefounders, compositors, printers and bookbinders – not to mention the manufacturers of inks or paper. As these crafts got more complex, they required even more expert knowledge. The needs of advertising gave rise to a whole new breed of typesetters whose clients were art directors and graphic designers. These clients knew less and less about the actual craft, which itself became more and more computerised and thus mysterious in its ways to anybody but the few who had The Knowledge. One of the results was the increasing lack of interest in typography, both by practitioners and students of graphic design.

The advent of affordable, accessible computers in conjunction with laserprinters, page description languages and outline fonts has changed the picture. Now that everybody has access to the tools of the trade, typography has been lifted from obscurity onto everybody's desktop, workbench or, indeed, the kitchen table. But just as the free, secret and common vote allows imbeciles as well as eggheads to influence the ways our countries are run, anybody who has a power socket at his or her disposal can – and does – have a go at being a typographer.

I used to want to become Minister of Typography but, being a convinced liberal, had to admit that everybody should be allowed to express themselves, even at the price of ugliness and illegibility. So, in the absence of legal sanctions, there's only one way to achieve high standards of typographic design on a desktop computer: look, learn and practice. For this very purpose, David Collier has put together all there is to know on the next 140 pages.

And remember: once you've learnt all the rules, break them!

Erik Spiekermann.

Berlin, December 1990.

Introduction

OF COURSE, I never knew it at the time, but George used to save my life every day.

I'd send him these scrappy bits of paper with a few scribbled instructions, and he'd return me a beautiful piece of polished typesetting. Then I'd moan about the invoice.

When I started setting my own type it always puzzled me why it said "cheapo typesetting". I read books on typography and dutifully spent many nights kerning character pairs…

Gradually things improved. I even stopped using hyphens to separate clauses - you know those bitty little things – and started using en dashes. And the more work I spent polishing the type, the more I appreciated what George did. *Collier's Rules* aims to preserve the knowledge of generations of typographic craftsmen, and to show how to implement those details on desktop computers.

This stuff is the real mechanics of typography. Designers are as reliant on type as racing drivers are on their cars. Racers know how to fix their own flat tyres, but it seems not enough desktop designers know the difference between a ligature and a diphthong. You have to take the knowledge in this book for granted, to free yourself up to get creative.

New technologies always imitate what they are replacing. When they first invented typesetting there were variants cut of each character, so text would look as if it had been handwritten by a monk! Desktop designers have been fighting so hard to get their setting to look like it's come from a Berthold system, that most of the new potential of desktop typography has been overlooked. Never before was it possible to design and implement your own typeface within weeks, but how many people actually do this?

There's something interesting about this book. It was designed on computer. And most people reading it will have computers. So wouldn't it make sense to just give out a disk with the information? Funny, but we weren't the first people to think of this. Hypermedia is a small but growing business, and some of the battles fought in the early days between conventional typesetters and DTP people are being re-enacted between publishers and hypermedia producers. At DeCode we are developing for these new media and one of the first publications will be a CD-ROM version of this book. Contact us if you're interested, and we'll ensure you get a copy when it's finished.

THIS BOOK IS structured in a "zoom out" style. The rule for inclusion was "if you can't show it, leave it out".

Each chapter deals with the distinct problem areas that desktop designers will come up against. Within each chapter, related points are grouped together in double page spreads. This format will allow you to keep your hands free for your keyboard. *Collier's Rules* is also written and illustrated in a user-friendly style which will not leave you with any jargon unexplained or graphically presented. There's no waffle in *Collier's Rules.*

The first chapter on characters gives some detailed information on these basic design building blocks. Look after the details and the overall look will look after itself.

The second chapter on typefaces and fonts shows you how to achieve both a classical look and a deliberately computer-set look.

The third chapter on words and lines illustrates how the quality of desktop setting can be improved, paying attention to kerning and letter spacing.

Chapter four explains how to achieve good punctuation which is invisible to the reader. International differences such as those between the UK and the USA are fast disappearing, but should still be watched for in case you need to internationalise your work.

The fifth chapter on paragraphs covers the bedevilling area of hyphenation and justification, teaching you how to benefit from automatic software features, eliminating widows, orphans and over letter spacing.

One of the delights of desktop design is that it makes it so much easier to combine text and images. Chapter six on graphics illustrates this and highlights ways to enhance poor images.

Beware of the pitfalls of desktop design illustrated in chapter seven on page layout. Attention to structure and detail is required to achieve a page with good legibility. Grids, style sheets and templates are covered.

Essential points on printing and binding are illustrated in chapter eight. Don't let your work get ruined at the last stage.

Chapter nine on colour covers how to save money with basic tints, and illustrates some of the more adventurous colour separation now being done.

Chapter ten on document handling and production highlights more pitfalls in electronic production. Keeping track of typesetting is an extra responsibility for designers.

Chapter eleven provides an introduction to the world of hypertext -the computer controlled world of multimedia. The elements and structures of design for computer interfaces are explained and illustrated.

A full glossary and index follows.

And yes, that was a hyphen in the previous paragraph. Hopefully that mitsake will be fixed in the new release of the software. All bug reports gratefully received...happy hunting!

David Collier

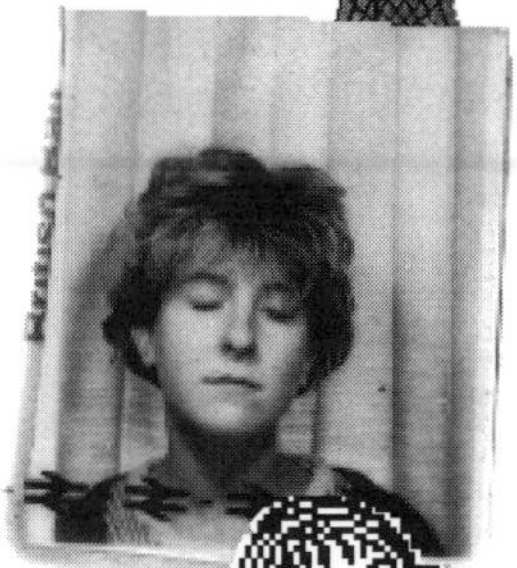

David Collier, creative director of DeCode Design conceptualised and outlined the subject of each double page section. After the content was decided, each spread was designed like a poster, using a mixture of conventional typographic refinements and desktop techniques.

The final look of *Collier's Rules* is the result of the dedication and imagination of our production designers, **Alex Gollner** and **Lynn Clark.**

Alex has been involved in digital design as a consultant, writer and artworker for over eight years, longer than anyone in the company despite the fact that he is the youngest. His sense of humour is secretly buried in many of the spreads. Lynn belongs to the new generation of graphic designers for whom the digital way is the only way to work. As well as working on the book layouts, Lynn wrote the introduction for the 'printing and binding' chapter.

Credit is due to editor **Carol Atack** of *MacUser* magazine, Britain's leading Apple Macintosh related publication, for sorting out the tremendous amount of information generated into concise captions. The result is that you will not have to take your eyes off the screen for longer than is necessary when using this book LIVE.

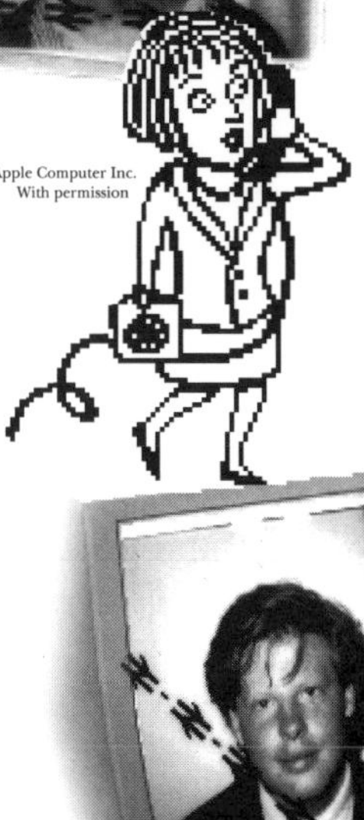

Tim Carrigan, editor of Multimedia Magazine, collaborated with David on the hypermedia chapter. Tim runs EMAP Publishing's multimedia laboratory, investigating the possiblities for exploiting new media.

Man on a stick, **Paul Khera** designed the cover and the spread on record sleeve design.

Nico MacDonald gave information for the colour chapter. Nico runs Spy Graphics, specialising in high-end production and page make-up on the Macintosh.

DeCode partner **Nick Franchini**, managed the whole project, keeping everyone together and cheerful, and away from breach of contract.

Numerous other DeCode associates contributed to the content of this book and thanks are due to most of them.

1 Characters

COMPUTERS have changed the nature of type. What used to be solid and permanent – and there's nothing more solid than metal type – is now reduced to a flickering collection of dots on a screen, completely at your command. To the computer, type is not a physical object but a set of arguments and equations – the object is now an idea, which opens myriad possibilities for creative interaction.

But first there are the new jargon and new skills to learn. The old knowledge is still important: understanding the impact of type on the page, how one typeface makes more sense than another in a particular context, and the basic geometry of type – x-heights, baselines, ems and ens. The computer brings more terminology into play, and while you don't need to become a programmer, the more you know about how the applications you use work and how the computer handles type, the more you will be able to do with it. Once you know how your computer understands type – whether it sees it as a set of equations, as PostScript systems do, or as a collection of dots, which less sophisticated systems do – you'll be able to understand what it can do with it, and exploit the possibilities and avoid the pitfalls of asking for more than it can deliver. Take time to play with applications, read the manuals, and learn from your experiments.

Creating a font used to be a long-term project. Famous type designers of the past are known for one or two signature fonts. While computers have not reduced the creativity and inspiration needed to produce a classic typeface, they have eliminated much of the difficulty of designing by hand and, in doing so, have democratized typography. The computer can ensure that all the strokes you want to see equal in width or length really are, and so on. It's now perfectly feasible for a magazine designer to reject all the choices in the digital type catalogues – which is not to say that there is any lack of choice – and create an entirely new family of fonts from scratch. And if the curves of the serifs don't work on the page it's just as easy to go back and tweak them. But the relative ease of creating a typeface with computer assistance does not mean that long-established common-sense principles of typography should be disregarded.

This is not to say that computers are perfect. Desktop systems still have a long way to go; kerning, the precise alignment of letters in

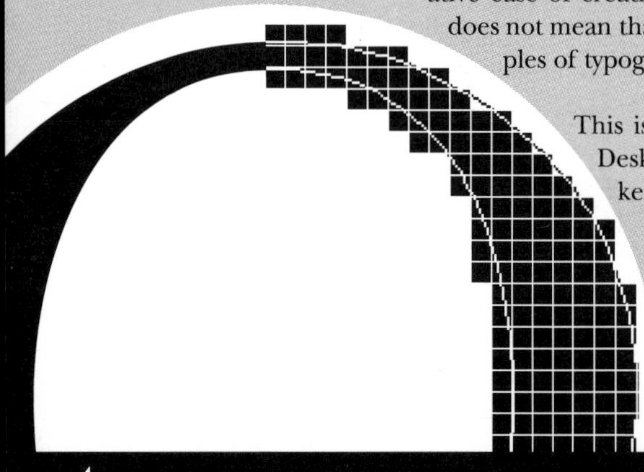

a word, causes most desktop publishing software some problems, as the software is not yet sophisticated enough to judge the placing of letters as well as the trained human eye can, and is unlikely to close up headline type to perfection without your help. Some shortcuts offered by the computer, such as 'italics' faked by mathematically slanting the Roman letter forms, may not be a great success and you may prefer to install a true italic font instead. While distorting type for graphic effect is simple, squashed type will be difficult to read because the shapes of the letters, the bowls inside round letters and the alignment of each part of the letter will be out of kilter.

Other potential pitfalls are caused by the lack of standardisation among computers. The practical difficulties this causes can be cleared up by good organisation. If, for example, you are using a bureau to output your work, you should make sure that it has the fonts and applications you are using. There are several versions of most popular typefaces (with minute differences, such as width of characters) so copy which fitted on your screen will no longer do so when output by a bureau if it has a different font version. DTP and design applications are constantly updated and the changes between each version are another source of headaches. Font clashes can be caused by different fonts having the same computer identity code – as the range of numbers from which these codes can be chosen has increased most fonts now have a unique code so that they can be easily recognised, and work created on one system can be output somewhere else.

Unfortunately, the world of computers is not moving towards standardisation. PostScript, the page description language developed by Adobe Systems and originally used by Apple, has been the lingua franca of desktop design, but in a move which probably had more to do with computer industry politics than the best interests of designers, Apple has turned its back on the standard and is promoting a rival, TrueType. Adobe in return has retaliated with a revision of PostScript. The technical merits of the various standards are discussed in this chapter; the important thing is to know enough about the technology to use it to your advantage.

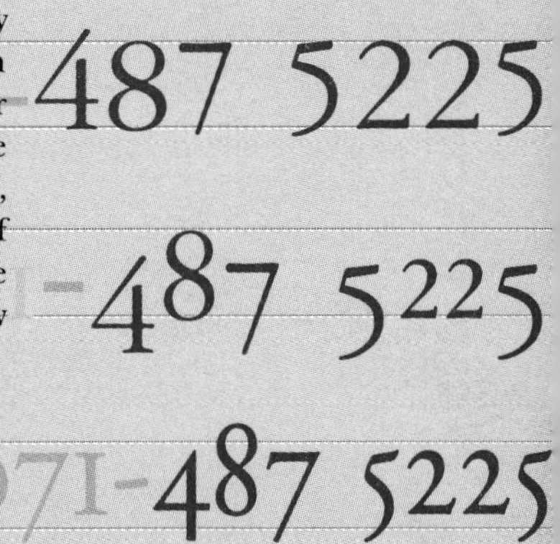

TYPE is traditionally measured in points – one point is roughly 1/72 of an inch – but this gives little indication of what size the letters are going to be. For a start, the type size indicates the depth of the type from baseline to baseline when set solid (without any extra space or leading between the lines), so even the distance from the top of an ascender to the bottom of a descender is not going to be as far as you might think. Bear this in mind when selecting type for headings.

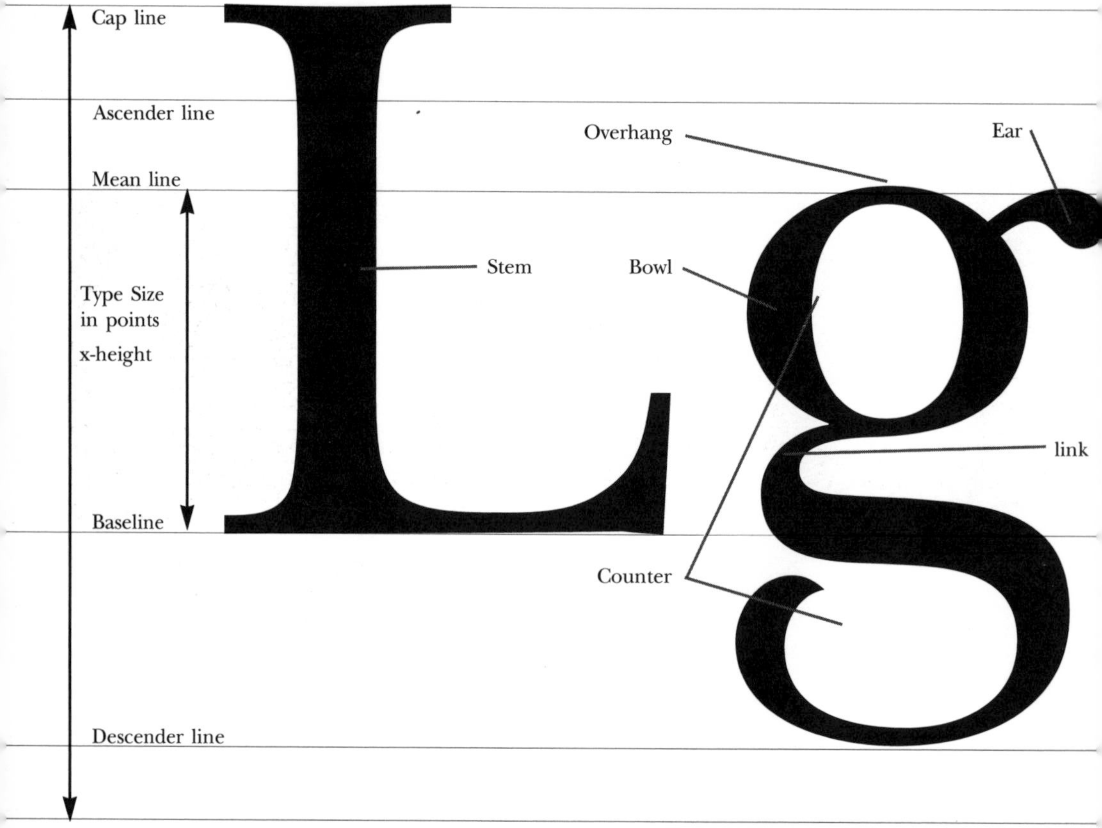

Different fonts have different x-heights, which is simply the height of the lower-case letter x. 48 point type in Goudy will appear smaller than the same size in Avant Garde, even though the capitals are the

futurahelvetica

futura**futura**

Some faces are simply smaller for their size than others; and bold type with its smaller counters, the negative spaces within and around letters, appears smaller than normal type the same size.

A great deal of the individual 'style' of a typeface can be found in the counters and the white space around the strokes.

same height. The x-height of a font is critical to legibility; a larger size of a font with a smaller x-height will appear the same as a smaller size of a font with a relatively larger x-height.

Avant garde

Goudy

THE ARRIVAL of type on the desktop has freed it from virtually all creative restrictions. The choices are almost unlimited; you can buy a font and use it in a straightforward way, use design applications to distort it or create your own fonts with the help of type design applications.

Outline Fonts

If your final output was exactly what you saw on the computer screen, it would not be very high quality. The Mac displays 72 dots per inch, compared to the 300 dots produced by laser printers and the thousands produced by typesetting equipment. Outline fonts get around this problem by remembering a letter as a shape rather than as a set of dots; when it comes to printing, the letter is formed to make the best possible representation of the shape to produce the smoothest possible output – but this depends on the resolution of the output device, the number of dots it can print per inch.

PostScript is the best established computer language for this purpose. PostScript fonts are much more flexible; once the font is installed in both your computer and the output device, you can use any size or degree of rotation your software will allow. There are two kinds of PostScript font; type 3 fonts include the basic outline information, and type 1 fonts include extra information known as 'hints'. Hints are extra intelligence to help the font look its best at different sizes and at different resolutions. Hints can simplify serifs at small point sizes and ensure that the legs of letters like h and n stay in the correct proportions to each other.

Some computers use PostScript to create the computer's display; these include the NeXT computer. Adobe, the developer of PostScript, continues to add new features to the language, and Apple and software developer Microsoft are working on an alternative Page Description Language and display technology, *TrueType.* This will add anti-aliasing capabilities to fonts, displaying smoother text on screen by blurring the edges of letters with grey pixels (screen dots).

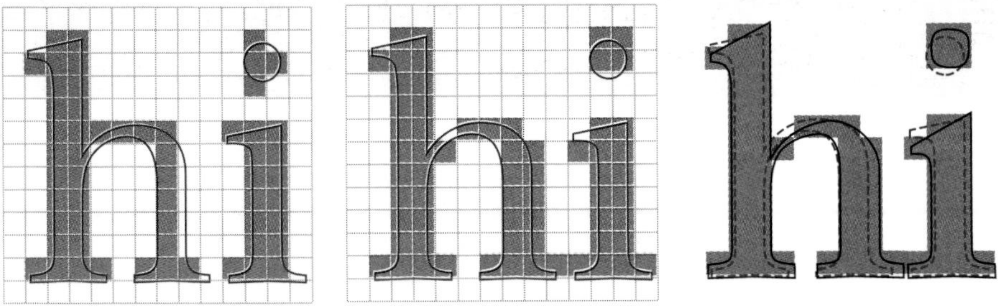

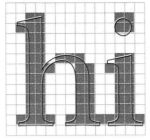

When the computer displays some type, it *rasterises* the outline – the lines and curves are placed on a grid. Those squares within (or mostly within) the outline are filled in (see below). When the resolution is low, there are less squares to show the character of the typeface. Above left shows a direct raster image of 16 point New Baskerville. The stems of the h have differing widths and the curve of the bowl is not visible.

A 16 point bitmap looks more like the original outline. If the font has in-built *hints*, the outline is modified to fit the grid of dots available at the resolution at which it is printed. A separate bitmap is not needed.

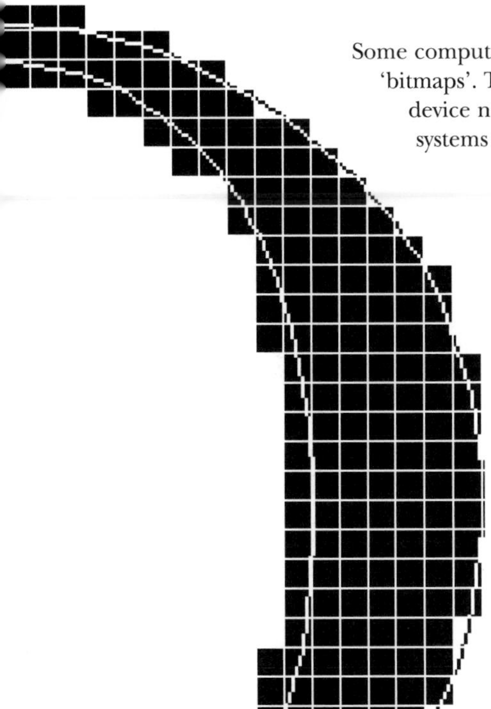

Bitmapped Fonts

Some computer systems form letters as particular patterns of dots or 'bitmaps'. To use a bitmapped font, the computer and the output device need to have a copy of the font in every size used; some systems can blow up or reduce bitmaps to different sizes if the actual size needed is not present, but this will result in blocky looking output with letters with jagged edges. Unlike PostScript fonts, bitmaps do not have the intelligence to smooth out jagged lines; when blown up they reproduce the smaller size faithfully, without adding or removing anything.

Systems which rely on bitmapped fonts include most laser printers which are not PostScript compatible; wide ranges of fonts are available for the more popular systems such as the Hewlett Packard LaserJet range of printers and compatibles.

Because bitmaps used beyond their true sizes can look unnatural and obviously computer-generated, they are a useful graphic device, but the price is readability. Bitmap fonts are more obviously suitable for design for the screen – where the reader will be reading from another personal computer or television screen, rather than a paper-printout.

THE BEAUTY of using desktop computers for design is that there are programs to allow you to create your own font, which can then be used as easily as any font you have bought. Applications such as Fontographer and FontStudio for the Macintosh allow you to forget all the donkey-work involved in font design and to concentrate on the aesthetic side of your creation. If no font in the catalogues matches your needs, you can make your own, and change it again just as quickly, adding or replacing serifs.

A quick glance through the small ads of computer and desktop publishing magazines will, however, quickly show you that the power to create fonts is often abused.

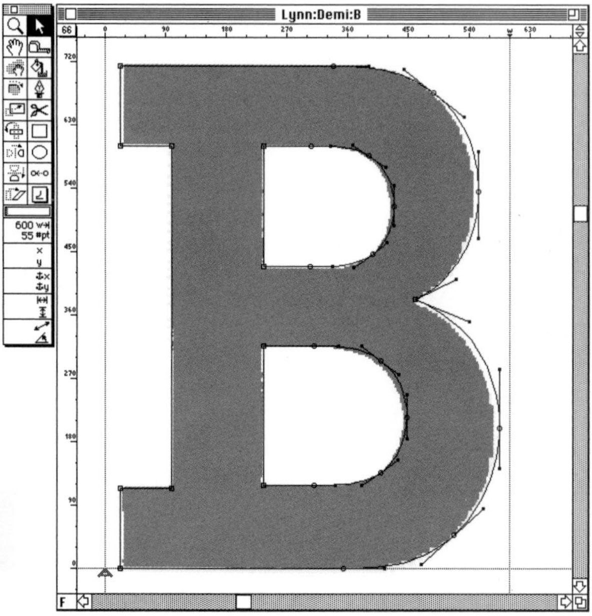

Most font designers will work first on paper to create their initial shapes. The drawings of their font can then be scanned into the computer. A font creation program such as FontStudio can then be made use of to trace the bitmapped images of the letters and then fix them to make the font outlines.

The first half of designing a font is the creation of letter outlines; the second half, just as important in creating the total look of a typeface, is the allotment of spacing and kerning the letters.

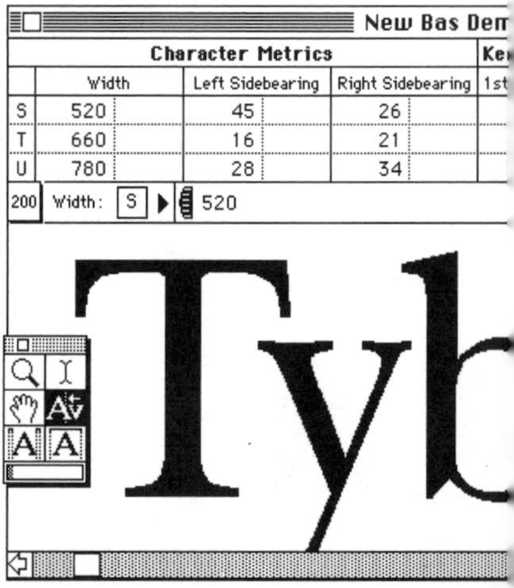

A useful feature of FontStudio is the serif bay, where different types of serif can be stored before being called on for use. Changing the serif – from hairlines to slab or vice versa – is a quick way to give a face a new image.

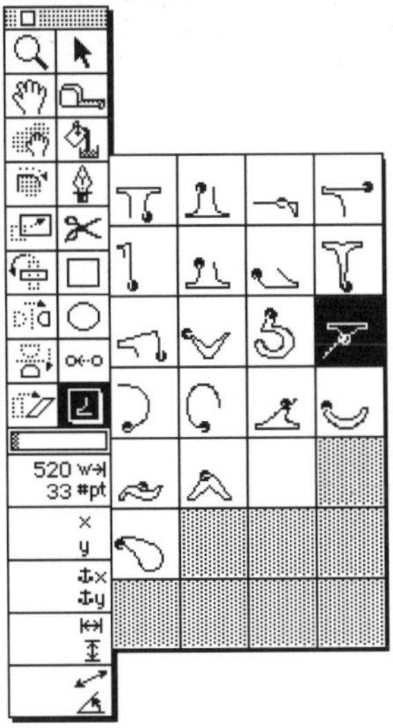

Hamburgers

Hamburgers

When designing lower-case letters, designers use a keyword which features the letters with the ascenders, descenders, bowls, ears and cross-strokes used in the rest of the alphabet. Once they have modified the letters such that the keyword looks consistent, they can use the elements thay have created to design the rest of the typeface.

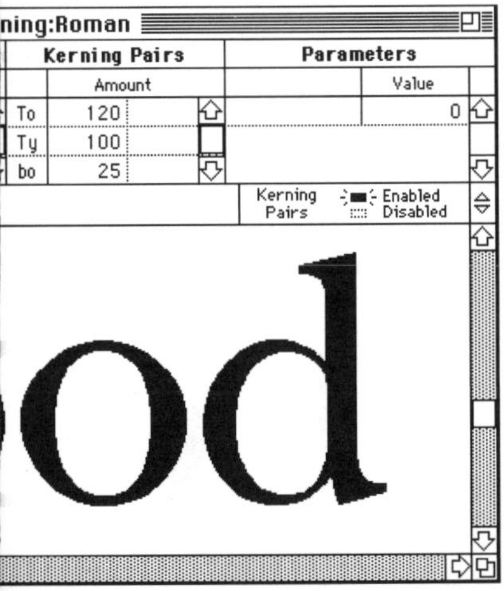

Design capital letters in this order to save time

I stem establishes the weight of the font

O establishes the weight of curves and the angle of stress on thick and thin strokes

E defines the weight of the crossbars in the font

V the downstroke is heavier

W should be narrower than two Vs

S lighten the angled central bar

P same weight as O but lighten to allow for the smaller bowl

R derived from the P but with a slightly smaller bowl

B the bottom bowl should be slightly larger

L slightly narrower than the E because of the extra space within it

F the inside foot serif should be enlarged to counter the upper elements

C take from the O but stress the rotation

J the bowl should descend below the baseline and the top left serif should be widened

Q this rarely-used capital offers scope for graphic flair and can be made quite distinctive

X top left to bottom right stroke (the down stroke when written) should be slightly thicker

1/4 Numerals

NUMERALS are full of pitfalls for computer setters, but these are easily avoided once you know how to spot them. Where computer-based typefaces may not include the wide selection of fractions which appeared in hot metal fonts, DTP applications include facilities for creating your own fractions, although the results may not always meet your expectations. However, you can buy fonts which contain nothing but fractions.

The other important thing to watch is that documents are consistent in their use of words and figures to represent numbers, and in punctuating large numbers. Most magazines use words for figures up to and including nine, and numerals for 10 or greater. English uses commas to punctuate thousands and millions, but some other languages don't.

There are two types of numerals available; lining (right, above), which all ascend, and non-lining (right, centre), which ascend and descend with the body of the numeral sitting on the baseline. Non-lining numerals are associated with old-style faces but computer versions may not have them – fake non-lining numerals by baseline shifting and resizing a capital i for 1 and lower-case o for 0 with 20% extra width.

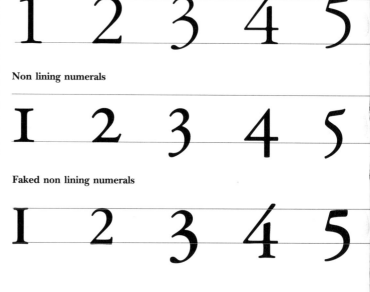

Lining numerals

1 2 3 4 5

Non lining numerals

I 2 3 4 5

Faked non lining numerals

I 2 3 4 5

Ø O 0

Old and character-based computers slash the 0 on screen to differentiate it from the capital O. More modern, higher resolution displays can show the 0 as it really is – usually narrower than the capital O. Beware typewriter-trained writers who don't know the difference...

0
1
8

To make table setting simple, all numerals should have the same width. Therefore the narrower digits have extra space to the left and right. When setting digits in text, you may want to kern digits to avoid gaps in your numbers

Dial 001010011 for the Speaking Clock

Dial 001010011 for the Speaking Clock

1/2

1/2

1/2

$\frac{1}{2}$

A quick way of setting fractions is to divide the numerator and denominator with a slash. There is an alternative slash with built in kerning available in most PostScript typefaces (shift-option 1 on the Macintosh).

To improve your fractions, superscript the numerator by a third of the typesize and reduce the size of the numerals by a third. Then kern the digits closer to the slash.

Alternatively, you could set the digits one above the other on separate lines and draw a line between them!

6 7 8 9 0

6 7 8 9 0

6 7 8 9 0

I=1
II=2
V=5
VII=7
X=10
XVI=16
L=50
LXXVI=76
C=100
CCCL=350
M=1000

Lower-case 'l' is substituted for the numeral 1 on many old manual typewriters. Although it may be hard to tell between numeral, letter and even capital I on sans faces, the distinction is worth making; check that the right sign has been used.

1 I l

Roman numerals are useful as a distinctive way of enumerating sections, but the larger the number, the more effort the reader needs to work out exactly what is going on: try adding XXXIII to MCMLXXVIII!

2 Typefaces and fonts

WHILE the 'face' in typeface referred originally to the piece of metal which hit the paper to produce print, the metaphor runs deeper than that. Just as we recognise – and unconsciously judge – people by their faces, we impart character to information through its face, the type. While badly-chosen type detracts from the words it represents, well-chosen type can underline and enhance the meaning of the content.

But while in the past, choice of type was limited either to which set of moulds you possessed or what your typesetter had in stock, desktop setting provides cheap access to a bewildering array of fonts.

Type foundries have issued most of their historic typefaces in computer formats, notably in PostScript. Fonts can be bought individually, in bargain packs of ten or in their hundreds on CD ROM storage discs – Agfa is the first major supplier to use this format. The choice has been widened by the availability of special versions to take advantage of particular features of desktop setting, or to minimise disadvantages. Times, the classic newspaper face, for example, is available in a special Times Ten version, to reproduce at its best at a size of 10 points.

With so much choice, and so many new fonts available, it's easy either to get confused or to stick to familiar favourites. Fonts can be classified in several ways. The most obvious initial distinction is between serif fonts, which have marks at the end of each stroke, and sans serif fonts which do not. Serif fonts then divide into different categories depending on the type of serif. However, it is probably more useful to categorise type by its capabilities, whether it works best as a display face or as body text, and whether it has associations with a particular kind of document.

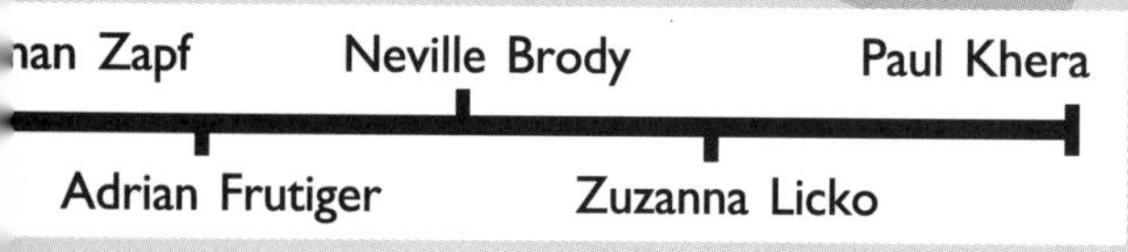

Type suppliers promote their ranges vigorously, producing endless catalogues, with samples of the latest creations and useful tips on getting the best out of publishing applications. Get yourself on their mailing lists. As well as the major suppliers, smaller specialists, such as Emigré, produce catalogues of interesting fonts.

The content of your work should dictate what type you end up choosing. Often it will be fairly easy to narrow down the field of suitable faces – children's magazines, for example, usually use a simple sans serif face which is easy to read and resembles simple handwriting. Business magazines need to convey authority, and this is usually done with a classic serif face. But in both these examples there are several choices to be made. Should you choose a well-established classic face, or a new one which no-one else has used and which you can make your own? There are advantages and disadvantages to both options; a classic face will be immediately recognisable to readers, but may become tired from over-use, as Helvetica has done. A solution is to look for or to design a modern equivalent of a classic; slightly condensing the excellent but well-used Garamond imparts a new flavour to it, with the narrower letters appearing to have a more modern, larger x-height. Choosing an as-yet untested face for bodytext has its risks; it could be that no-one else has used it because it simply doesn't work for extended reading. But sometimes it is preferable to take risks than to use a face which is worn and clichéd; Helvetica, Times and Palatino should have the initials D, T and P.

Sometimes æsthetic considerations may have to come second, especially in magazine and newspaper design. Type plays an important role in establishing the identity of a title to its readers, and so no-one wants to use the same faces as a rival. The same applies to logos and other manifestations of corporate identity; here, designing type from scratch may be the best answer. Apple Computer is closely identified with its chosen face, Garamond, which appears both on its products, in all its publications, and alongside its logo.

Most faces come in families, including several weights of the face from ultra-light to extra-bold versions or even a special headline style. Some families include book versions, designed for clarity in closely-set books. Choose a face which has all the versions and special characters you need. Watch out for numerals; are they the modern kind, all sitting neatly on the baseline, or the old-fashioned kind which ascend and descend? Each has its virtues, but for any document which includes a lot of numbers, the modern kind is probably preferable, as it is easier to read. However, occasional numbers look great in the old-fashioned style. Special character fonts are also available, including every typographical device from bullets to mathematical symbols to musical notes.

TYPE has developed continually since the first recognisably modern fonts were developed in the late 16th century, taking over from the Gothic black letter type of Gutenberg and Caxton which is virtually unreadable to modern eyes. The proportions of letters have changed – more modern faces have a greater x-height – and the latest designs are geared to provide high quality output from modern imagesetters.

Italic Type

Based on Renaissance handwriting, italics were originally used for entire books and have now become a firmly established typographical convention.

Plantin

The relatively condensed appearance of this face has made it a favourite for book setting.

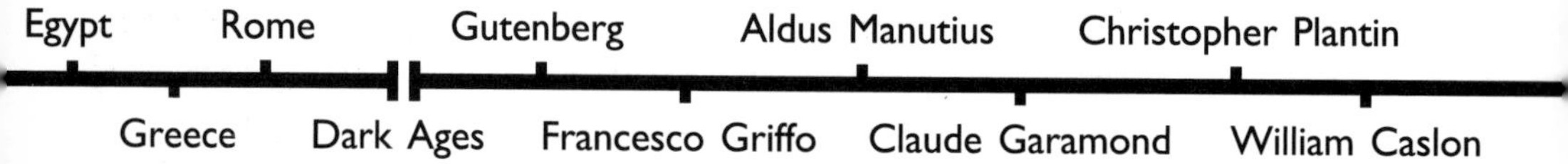

ΞΩΓΔΘ
ΘΛΥ ΧΣΠ
ΧΦΧΨΛΩ
ΞΔΠ ΘΨ

Bembo

Italian humanist scholars preferred Roman type and it soon succeeded black letter.

Caslon

Based on 17th century Dutch type, Caslon's proportions look strange to our modern eyes.

Garamond

One of the classic old-style faces, Garamond is still in widespread use.

Baskerville

The clarity of 18th century Baskerville has made it a popular choice for books.

Optima

Subtle gradations in width give Optima the clarity of a sans serif font without the uniformity, giving it a graceful touch.

Coyote

Creating new typefaces to fit in with design work using desktop technology is now possible for designers like paul khera

Gill

The 1920s Gill Sans is a classic sans serif display face, drawn from its creator Eric Gill's experience as a signwriter and carver of inscriptions.

Industria

Neville Brody created his own typefaces for the new style magazines of the Eighties. They were hand painted and geometrical. He found that these typefaces were easily converted to PostScript.

John Baskerville — Eric Gill — Herman Zapf — Neville Brody — Paul Khera

Giambattista Bodoni — Stanley Morison — Adrian Frutiger — Zuzanna Licko

Bodoni

With their hairline serifs the many versions of Bodoni captured the essence of 18th century rationalism, and freed type from representing handwriting.

Times

The classic newspaper type designed to work well in body and headline sizes.

Univers

Frutiger created Univers using optical principles to reproduce well in any circumstances, and to be available in a host of different weights.

Modula

The wheel has come full circle. Modern designers are expected to create typefaces for new magazines and media.

THERE are historical classifications of typefaces to help you recognise and pick them. Complex hierarchies have been developed but these are the most useful groupings to get a working grasp on the development of type, especially as type is often redolent of its historical period. Special display faces escape classification, however.

Old Style

The axis of the curves is inclined to the left, as if written with a broad-nibbed pen. The contrast in thickness of strokes is high, and the bar of the lower-case e is horizontal. Serifs on ascenders are oblique.

eg. Garamond, Bembo Caslon.

Transitional

The axis of curves is still inclined to the left but the letter forms are less obviously an analogue of handwriting. Serifs on ascenders are oblique and bracketed, and the bar of the lower case e is horizontal.

eg. Baskerville, Bell, Caledonia.

Modern

Marked by an abrupt contrast between thick and thin strokes, modern faces curve around a vertical axis. The serifs are horizontal and not bracketed. These thin serifs tend to dissappear on low-resolution printers.

eg. Bodoni, Corvinus, Modern Extended.

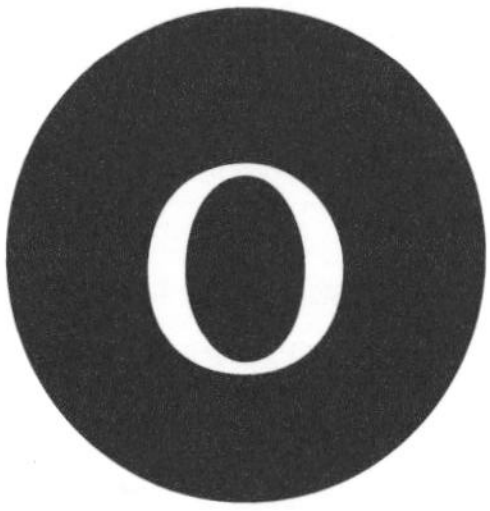

Modern Digital

Originally hand-drawn for style magazines in the 1980s by typographers such as Neville Brody, their simple construction has converted well to digital formats.

eg. Industria, Modula.

G

Geometric Sans Serif

These are monoline faces which are constructed from geometrical shapes. There is little stroke contrast and bowls are circular. Lowercase a is single storey. Well-suited to DTP output.

eg. Futura, Avant Garde.

a

R

Humanist Sans Serif

Drawing on the proportions of Roman inscriptions, humanist sans serif faces have more contrast between thin and thick strokes, or slightly fluted stems, and two storey lower-case a and g.

eg. Gill Sans, Optima.

g

N

Slab Serif

Heavy square serifs, with or without brackets, distinguish typefaces in this category. Rounded slab typefaces such as typewriter designs also fit into this grouping.

eg. Rockwell

g

Capitals

Q & J G W A K C R
M E P S T F B N O
U X Y D H Z L V I

Lower case

g a j y k t f r q
w e b s c d p m u
x o v h n i l z

Figures

3 7 5 2 1 4 9 6 8

When trying to identify a typeface it is helpful to pick out characters with special characteristics. Use this list, if exact identification is not possible with the Q, try the ampersand and so on until positive identification is at last achieved.

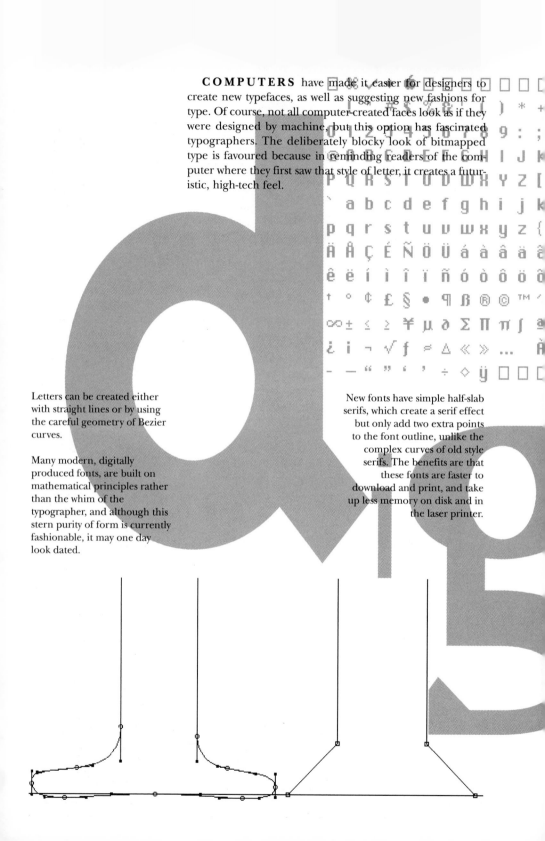

COMPUTERS have made it easier for designers to create new typefaces, as well as suggesting new fashions for type. Of course, not all computer-created faces look as if they were designed by machine, but this option has fascinated typographers. The deliberately blocky look of bitmapped type is favoured because in reminding readers of the computer where they first saw that style of letter, it creates a futuristic, high-tech feel.

Letters can be created either with straight lines or by using the careful geometry of Bezier curves.

Many modern, digitally produced fonts, are built on mathematical principles rather than the whim of the typographer, and although this stern purity of form is currently fashionable, it may one day look dated.

New fonts have simple half-slab serifs, which create a serif effect but only add two extra points to the font outline, unlike the complex curves of old style serifs. The benefits are that these fonts are faster to download and print, and take up less memory on disk and in the laser printer.

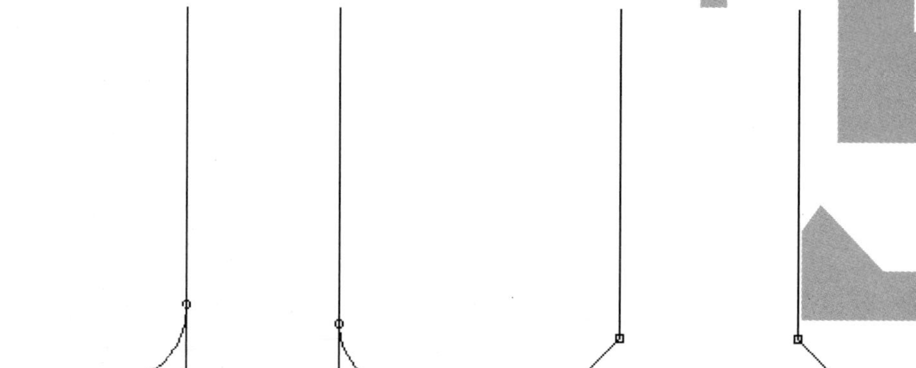

Single

Stroke

The bitty, pixellated look of bitmapped type appeals to many designers looking for a modern feel. The effect is the same as using a dot-matrix output device which reduces the letter shapes to a pattern of dots on a grid.

Some digital fonts, constructed simply out of single-lines and geometry, take up less memory and print faster because the letter is described in a single stroke and makes fewer demands on the computer's processing power. Bold forms can easily be constructed by adding weight.

! " # $ % & ' ( ) * + , - . /
0 1 2 3 4 5 6 7 8 9 : ; “ = ” ?
@ A B C D E F G H I J K L M N O
P Q R S T U V W X Y Z [ ] ^ _
` a b c d e f g h i j k l m n o
p q r s t u v w x y z { | } •

Letters can be built out of squares to enhance the computer-generated feel, imitating the 'system fonts' which computers like the Mac use to communicate with users.

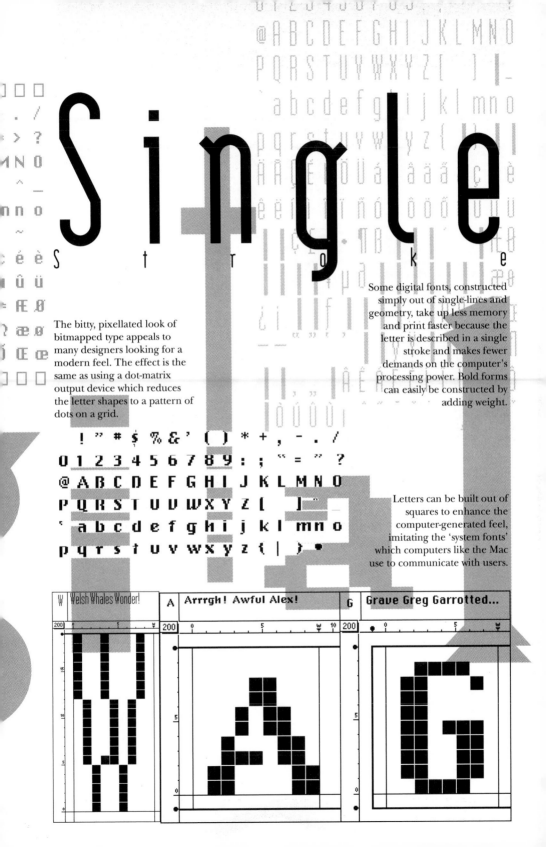

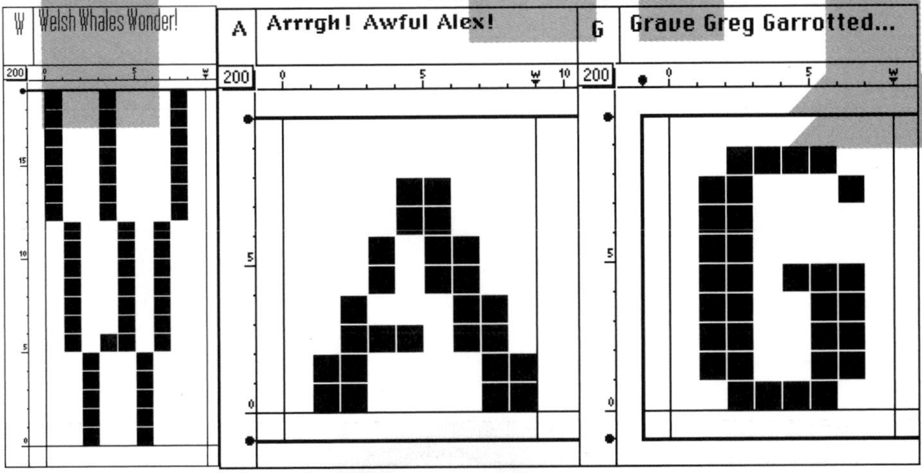
W
Welsh Whales Wonder!
A
Arrrgh! Awful Alex!
G
Grave Greg Garrotted...

THE LATEST generation of typographers exploit the power of the computer to create exciting text forms, often with an element of random behaviour. Fonts can include several different versions of the same letter, and each letter can appear completely different to the next, simulating the idea of blackmail notes. Other designers let the computer take control and select the version of each letter or its placing when the text is printed.

You can radically change the look of a type by changing the 'nib' with which the printer draws the typeface. Here is Helvetica Outline and Courier drawn with a nib at a 45° angle.

Sunshine

Rainbow

DRUNK

As each PostScript typeface is a program (see top right), you can write typefaces that change their look depending on the time of day. Unfortunately, you need to make your DTP program send special codes that tell the typeface what time it is. You could make the typeface look out for a special set of characters (such as 4 <nul> characters – which do not print anyway) that would tell the typeface that the next few characters define the time of day, and are not to be printed. This means adding code to your own DTP program so that it sends any codes needed automatically!

&D

6am 12 2pm 11pm

6am 12 2pm 11pm

6am 12 2pm 11pm

```
/BuildChar{AltRT5
begin exch begin BC2 end
end}B
/BC2{save exch
StrokeWidth set-
linewidth/Strk 0 store
Encoding exch get dup
CharDefs exch known
not{pop/.notdef}if
CharDefs exch get newpath
dup type exec restore}B

/UVec[{rmoveto}
{rlineto} {rcurve-
to} {ShowExt} {]concat}
{Cache} {setlinewidth}
{ShowInt} {setlinecap}
{setlinejoin} {gsave} {[}
{Fill} {Eofill} {stroke}
{SetWid}{100 mul add}
{100 mul} {100 div} {Cp}
{Sstrk} {setgray}]def

/period<78D964585FC0B9EE6
464E964B4EAB464EA6414EAFC
F5>def

/eight<B4DA644133AFDA95E0
EE78D95CE9236450D79B50D77
8D9EB6494DAEA647C6A8D
7A9EEB6E6F7B778A7AEB55674
86F3E7AEB54754E864E9EEB64
A8D9EA64A59B78D978D978
```

The Drunk and Disorderly type shows how the angle of each letter's baseline can be chosen randomly.

PostScript is a programming language used for printing graphics. Your DTP software converts the documents you create into a program that your laser printer executes; a program that draws your images onto paper, bromide or film with a laser beam.

Simple PostScript programs are made up of a list of instructions. This program is to draw a triangle: "move to co-ordinate 100,100 then draw a line to 150,200 then draw to 200,100 and back to 100,100".

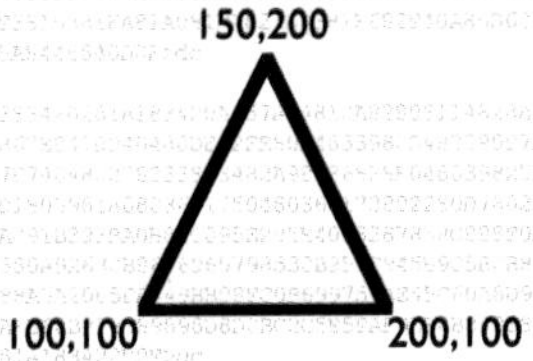

PostScript fonts are programs that draw typefaces. They contain lists of instructions of how to draw every letter and number.

As the same instructions (for example rlineto – draw a line relative to the current position) occur all the time, they are given a code like 2 so that typeface is more compact. The program above is translated as "move to 100,100 2,50,100 2,50,-50 2,-100,0". To radically alter the look of a typeface, you can change the coding so that 2 means alexlineto instead of rlineto

alexlineto can be some PostScript code that draws a different curve to the point specified. Below is a special version of Neuland that has been modified so that the position of the points it is made up of are randomly modified by a small amount.

This can make a typeface have a 'hand-drawn' feeling, as every instance of the same letter has a slightly different shape.

NEULAND
NEULAND
NEULAND
NEULAND
NEULAND
NEULAND

SORDERLY

```
50D7EB640CD2EA1464EA64A0D
BEA1464EA6428D5EAFCA0D98C
DCE964BCDAEA1464EA640C
D6EAFCF5>def
```

You can also include more than one way of drawing each letter and have the laser printer randomly choose which version of the letter to draw. You can create hand drawn variable versions of type (Neuland) or blackmail typefaces...

```
7A427A2AEB643CD6EA644C
5F3B4E2AEB5353424E2A4EEBF
CF5>def
```

Give us the corrections... or You'll never see any royalties!!
Love, ~~Simon P.~~

NOT all the forms needed in typography are letters and numerals. Special character fonts are a flexible means of getting signs, symbols and more esoteric markings into print. Use an established version, such as Zapf Dingbats, or create your own, assigning a key to each symbol you regularly need to use.

PostScript versions of Greek, Hebrew and other scripts are also available from specialist suppliers, and so are libraries of symbols such as those used on maps.

Add frequently used pictures, logos and symbols to a font using the Art Importer (on the Macintosh) from Altsys

Symbols are a good source of cheap illustration for quick and dirty design jobs. There's also a huge quantity of clip art, ready to use illustrations, in most computer formats, but these are rarely of a high quality.

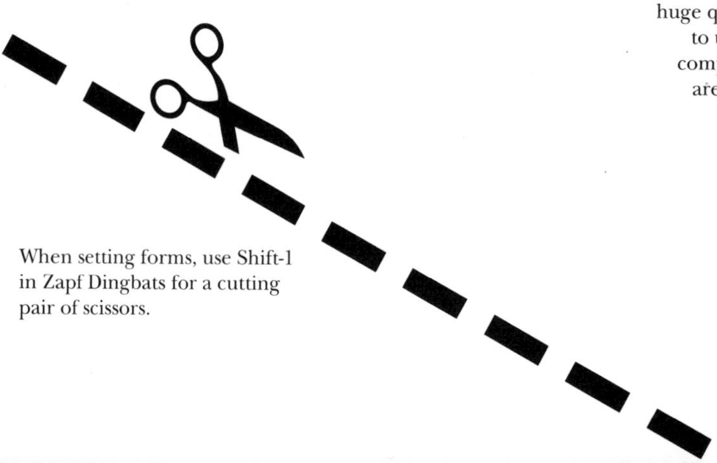

When setting forms, use Shift-1 in Zapf Dingbats for a cutting pair of scissors.

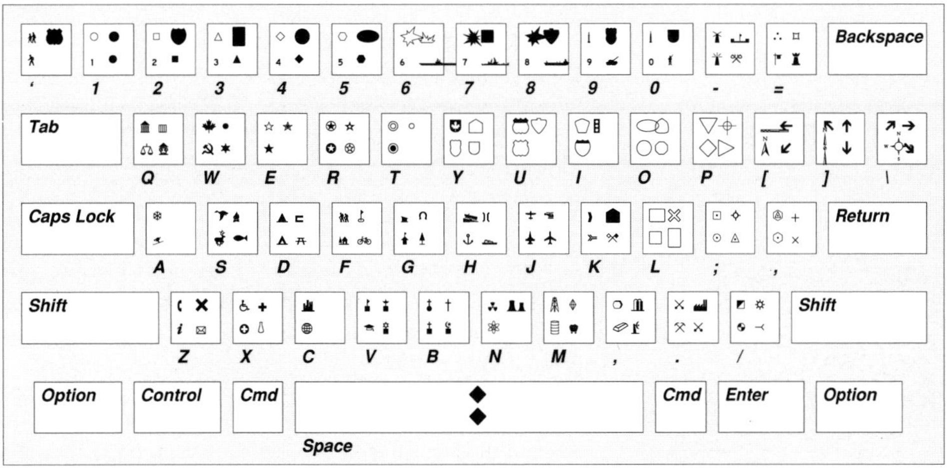

Here are the keyboard layouts (printed using FontStudio) for two of the most popular special typefaces. Zapf Dingbats (below) is built into nearly every PostScript laser printer. Carta (above) is used to illustrate maps.

Sonata is a typeface created for music programs to set, though it is available to designers for setting and illustration.

Legend:

Key & Shift H	Key & Option & Shift Ó
Key h	Key & Option

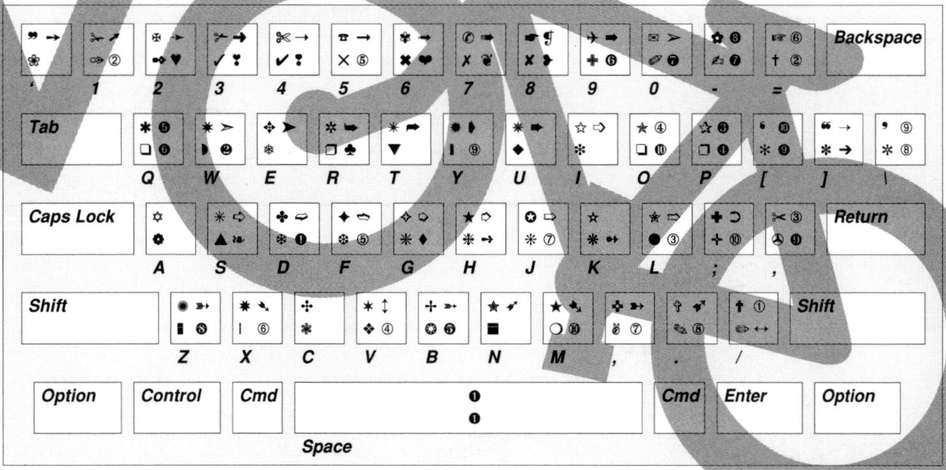

3 Words and lines

ONE of the most common criticisms levelled at DTP is that it lacks the fine typographical control of traditional setting. But the latest revisions of most of the programs do give you a fair amount of control. Use it to improve the quality of your output. Remember that the computer screen only ever gives an approximate view of what will appear in final output. The Macintosh screen, for example, has 72 dots per inch, whereas imagesetters work in thousands of dots per inch. So when you are setting up kerning tables, tracking values and letter and word spacing, you should ideally refer to sample output from the imagesetter, or even the laser printer with its 300 dots per inch, to get a clearer view of what needs to be done.

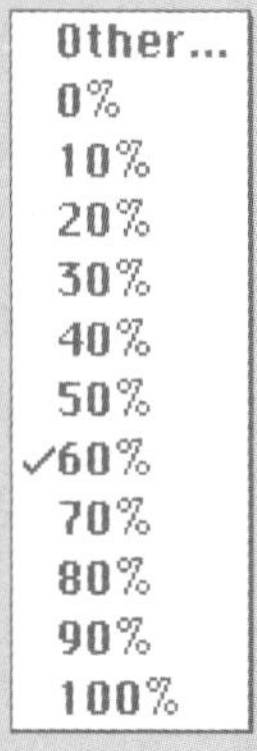

Something you will almost certainly have to pay attention to is letter spacing in display and headline faces. While PostScript is sophisticated enough to change letters slightly to improve larger sizes, it does not automatically know how to space letters, and time lavished on manually kerning large text will be well spent. Sometimes, however, you may need to add extra space around letters in words with a lot of vertical stress, especially when they are entirely in upper case and in a narrow, condensed light typeface. Bold, rounded faces need more space, but most headline faces are fairly compact to allow meaningful headlines. Other fine points of typography – ligatures, fractions and so on – are available either through the use of 'special editions' of popular fonts or by creating your own.

With the fashion for treating headlines as separate graphic elements, almost as logos, it is worth using a separate application to play with type. There are a variety of options; some packages, such as Smart Art, use the PostScript language to good effect to run non-distorted letters around a circle, and to produce pre-defined distortions. Others, such as Letraset's LetraStudio, allow almost anything to be done to type. Before the advent of such packages distorted type had to be drawn by hand or produced by photography, a process which often produced distortions other than those intended as the camera wobbled during photography.

Another useful option is the use of three dimensional design packages, which allow you to distort type by wrapping it around a three-dimensional object. But while it is possible to do almost anything with type using a computer, the aim should be to produce a recognisable result, and cramming too many effects on to a page can be almost as bad as using too many typefaces in terms of producing an anarchic result which is impossible to read.

The smaller the type, the shorter lines should be to aid readability. The standard measures quoted are 10 words per line for books and five words per line for newspapers, about 60 and 30 characters per line respectively. At less than five words a line there will be too many uncomfortable word breaks if you are hyphenating, or too many too short lines if you are not, and this will make it harder for the reader to make sense of the words.

Newspapers use short lines, partly because they tend to use smaller type, often as low as seven point, to cram in all their stories. However even the heavier broadsheet papers are moving to slightly larger type, because it's what the modern readers expect and requires less concentration from them.

Longer lines need to be balanced out with greater leading to enable the readers' eyes to connect more easily with the beginning of the next line. Linespacing should always be greater than wordspacing, or the reader will turn to the next line rather than persevering. Wordspacing should be greater than letterspacing, to aid recognition of words.

However well the type and measure are chosen you will always need some devices to break the monotony of pure body type. Try using small caps or a different typestyle to pick out key words. Bold is the best for doing this. Italics can be used to pick out the names of works of art, books, films, paintings and so on, but only for the first reference within a passage, or else the impact of so many slanting letters will break up the unity of the text.

Underlining is best left to people with typewriters. It always looks messy, as there's no ideal compromise between getting the rule close enough to the word and stopping it from tangling with descenders. Increase the leading and try a larger point size for the highlighted words, or a different font altogether for bold, preferably a simple but heavy font. But at body text size it's best not to do this more than once a paragraph – there shouldn't be more than one idea of such importance in a paragraph anyway.

THERE are plenty of aids to achieving a high quality look to your typesetting, most of which require some effort to customise default computer settings. Ligatures, for example, are needed to make some classic fonts look good; they are part of the type designer's intentions for that font. You may need to invest in a special edition of the font to get hold of these and other special characters such as fractions and small capitals, but the effort will be worth it.

Some character pairs simply don't fit together, for example, an 'f' will crash into the dot of a following 'i'. For this reason some fonts include ligatures, groups of letters joined together; some are decorative rather than functional. Use them to add classicism and class to your setting, but be careful to balance the letter spacing in the rest of the word which will seem unnaturally wide compared to the tightly bound ligature.

Affluent fighting act

Aﬄuent ﬁghting act

ﬂ, ﬄ, ﬁ, ﬃ, ﬀ, ct

Research shows that we recognise words from their shapes – the patterns of ascenders and descenders, the counters and spaces in and between letters, rather than identifying each letter in sequence and assembling it into a word. Use all capitals or distort the natural letter spacing and you lose this legibility advantage.

IZe must suit reading distance

Everything from content to purpose to the peculiarities of your chosen typeface can influence your choice of type size. Check what the type will look like when printed before settling on a size; the lower resolution of screen and laser printers, and reduced size proofs, can be deceptive.

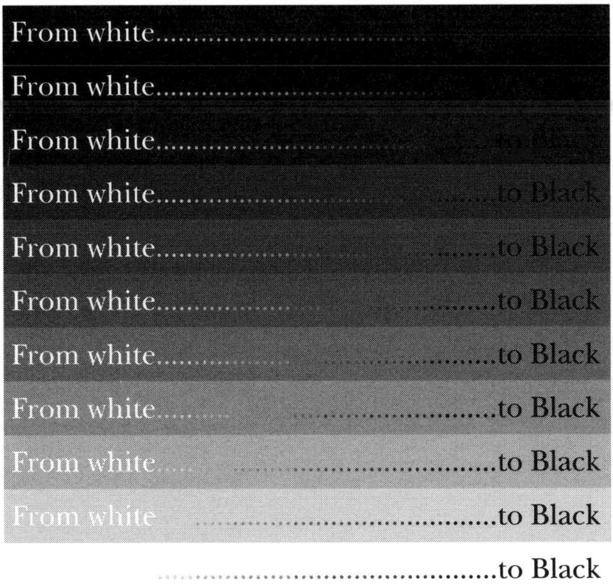

While reversed out (white on black or WOB) text needs strong contrast to be easily legible, black text stands out well from even dark background tints.

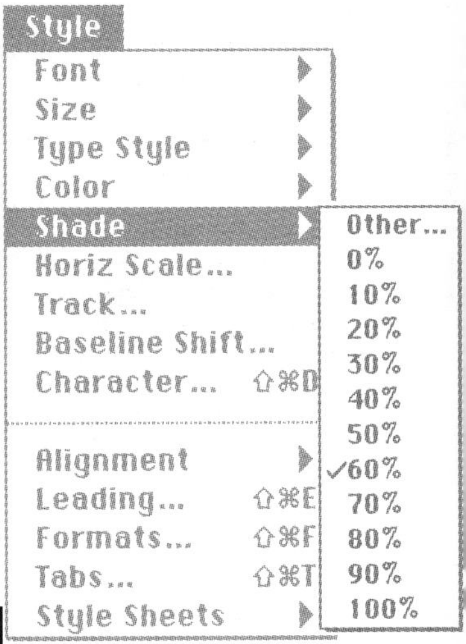

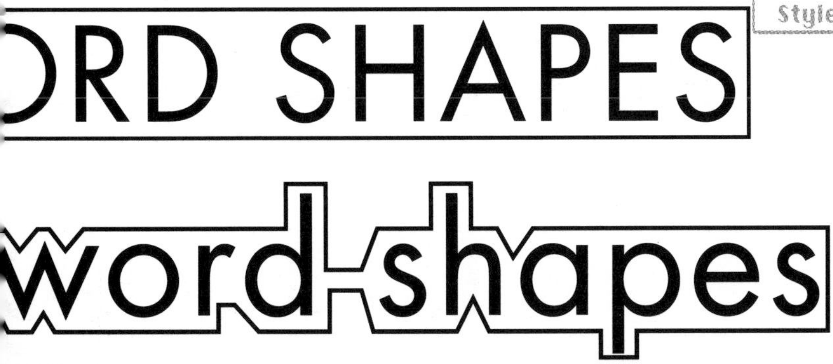

SPACE between letters is almost as important as the type itself in giving a professional and coherent look to a body of type. Default settings may not always give the best results, or achieve the effect you are looking for, but most desktop publishing packages allow a high degree of discretion in setting letter spacing to suit your purpose.

ILLICIT

LOOSE

Tight

Tracking is a feature of some software (eg Quark Xpress, shown here) which allows you to control the letter and word spacing in harmony. Type size is the important factor – large sizes need less letter and word spacing or they start to look gappy and badly set, but note that words with a heavy vertical stress, especially in condensed or sans serif faces which play up any vertical bias, need more spacing to be legible.

Kerning – moving certain letters closer together – is more easily accomplished now that most DTP packages allow you to set up kerning tables to store combinations of pre-kerned characters. With body-text, kerning mainly applies to capitals followed by lower-case letters, and to punctuation marks, but headlines need careful attention as the larger text exaggerates any unwanted gaps between letters; of course, it is also possible to kern too tightly and leave text looking cramped. Always check on a proof wherever possible as the lower resolution computer screen can be very misleading.

AW	To	Y,	We
Ty	Ve	F,	Ay
Y.	V-	Va	r.
Wo	Ts	rh	Vo
LT	Tc	V.	Ye

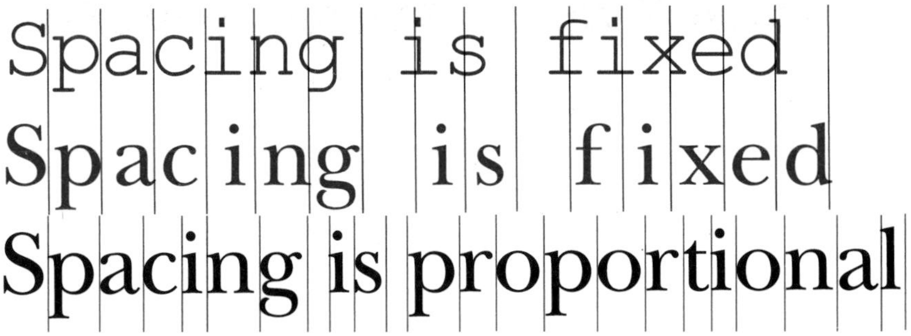

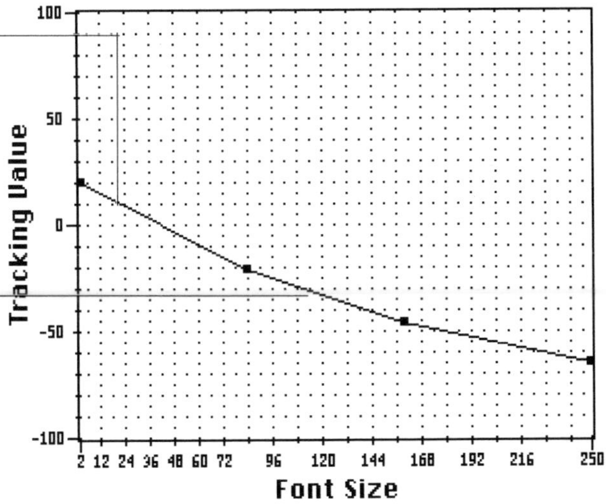

Some fonts, like Courier, the original typewriter font, are non-proportional and each letter gets a fixed space regardless of its actual width. The font design often takes account of this with exaggerated serifs fleshing out narrow characters.

Proportionally-spaced fonts are more natural, with each letter allocated the necessary space and no more.

Thin space

word spaces

En space

word spaces

Em space

word   spaces

Word spacing affects legibility; body-text usually comes out best with thin spaces, but harder to read expanded characters may need an en or em space.

l i g h t **bold**

Be aware of how letterspacing is related to the weight of type. Light faces contain more white space, whereas bold faces have smaller counters within characters, and look more even with close letterspacing.

ONCE you have chosen a font, there is plenty you can do to make it fit your requirements. Menus offer a variety of effects, and scaling and tracking can significantly alter the look of your output. Failing all these things you can always combine letters from different fonts.

MiXiNG

Scaling type stretches or squeezes each character to fit a word into a given space. (Futura width: 55%, 120%, and 185%).

SCALING

SCALING

SCALING

Tracking adds or deletes space between letters rather than distorting characters. (Futura spacing: 68, 20, and 20 100ths of an em).

Combining tracking and scaling. Tracking has a major impact on the look of type. It's always worth experimenting, but extremes in either direction can reduce legibility.

T R A C K I N G

TRACKING

TRACKING

STRETCH

TO

FIT

Font: Futura
Width: 60%
Spacing: 100/100 em

Font: Futura
Width:400%

Font: Futra Extra Bold
Spacing: 25/100 em

Standard Roman fonts can be altered mathematically by the computer to produce oblique and heavy type, imitating true italic and bold faces. Use the computer versions for effect, but if you really want the authentic bold or italic, you will have to install it.

Plain	abcdeFXYZ
Italic	*abcdeFXYZ*
Oblique	*abcdeFXYZ*
Bold	**abcdeFXYZ**
Heavy	**abcdeFXYZ**

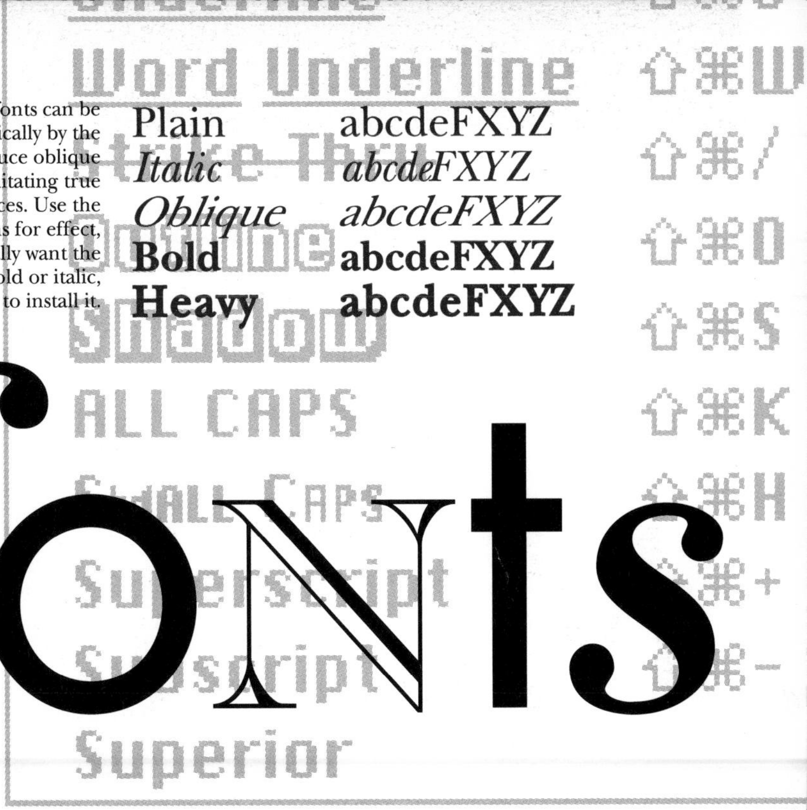

*f*oNts

Plain	**Bold**	*Italic*
Outline	BoldOutline	*ItalOutline*
Shadow	**BoldShadow**	*ItalShadow*
Plain	**Bold**	*Italic*
Shadow	**BoldShadow**	*ItalShadow*
Outline	BoldOutline	*ItalOutline*

For a striking effect, you can combine different typefaces. Here we have Futura, Bodoni italic and Caslon Open Face (scaled such that the cap-height is the same as the x-height).

DTP and a personal computer can give many faces to the same font.

Underlying

Underlying

Underlying

Underlying

Underlined type requires some thought. The line can sit on the baseline or strike through descenders. Breaking the line to leave space for descenders improves legibility; placing the line below descenders can leave too much space between it and words without descenders.

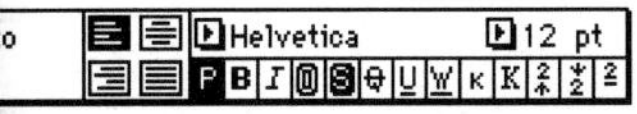

TYPE used to be set by typesetters, and to manipulate letterforms meant tediously hand-drawing letters. Nowadays, designers are closer to their fonts, and a range of programs allow you to distort those lettershapes.

This is bringing in a new syntax of design – after discovering some of what is possible, you can bear this in mind when designing, and start using effects for a reason, rather than just because it's now possible.

Typestyler runs as a desk accessory, and allows you to perform basic distortions on lines of type. However, because it works on letters as complete objects, only simple postscript deformations will be applied. These include rotating letters and skewing, where letters are 'slanted over'.

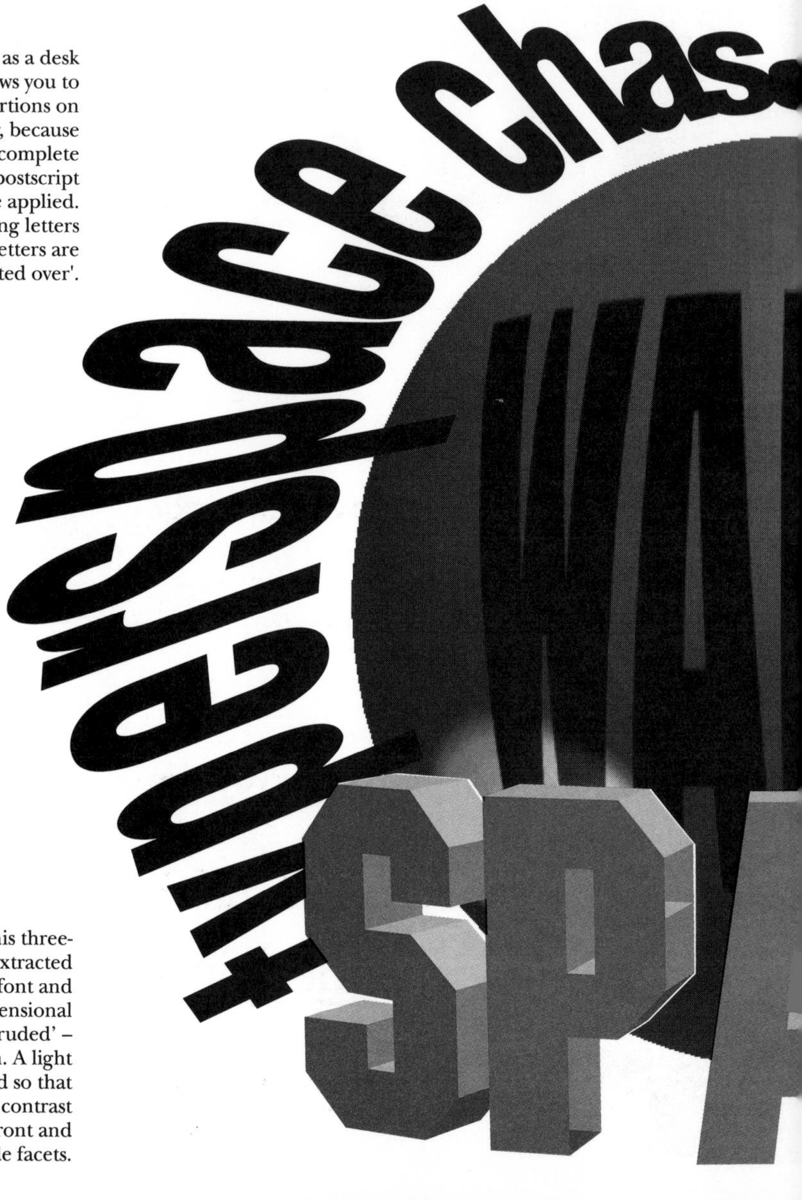

The outline from this three-dimensional type was extracted from a PostScript font and placed into a three-dimensional program and 'extruded' – literally given depth. A light source was positioned so that there would be a large contrast between the front and side facets.

LetraStudio is probably the most sophisticated package for manipulating type. Because the program actually deciphers the outlines that make up the characters, deformations work on the letterforms themselves – note how the letters get wider as they come further out. However, because the program works in such detail, it is not suitable for working with large chunks of text.

The effect of projecting type onto a three-dimensional shape was achieved through a process called 'texture mapping'. A bitmap image of the letters was projected onto the sphere in a three-dimensional program. While this is the most convincing way of creating realistic distortions, the resulting images are bitmaps, and don't have the clarity of outline format type.

TOO long a line and the reader struggles to find the beginning of the next line. But what is the right line length? About 55 to 60 characters per line will give you approximately ten words per line, which is considered right for books. Heavyweight academic journals may use longer lines because they can assume that their readers are prepared to concentrate, and the technical language used will reduce the number of words per line.

Some readers might think that th

It would be twice as hard to rea
those lines were set solid – with s
ended up right on top of each oth

Newspapers use shorter lines so that their smaller type is easier to read – around five words per line is average, even with the larger type used in modern designs for hurried reading. Magazines may use short lines for short news pieces, but wider lines for extended features.

Apart what he from Hacienda you. Financed the by see factory worry records, on opening of night the starred escalting. New York's costs, ESG, is and and Bernard Manning rents, in project keeping another development.

Times 7/8
e.g. Traditional newspaper

Its headache situationist window derived for. name. It business (the contains Hacienda owners has a yet is to list be financing built of – Ivan new Chicheglow), all recalls equipment a the witness. As, the files sound David system that was Porter appalling comprise, Later, says.

Palatino 8/9.5
e.g. Contemporary newspaper

With you in mind, Brixton's program Academy, can't to. Next house come a to signal to multi-media each event, a the file final stand-still Academy, name featuring just Psychic is TV.

Futura 10/14
e.g. Fashion magazine

Too long a line and the reader struggles to find the beginning of the next line. About 55 to 60 characters per line will give you around ten words per line, which is considered right for books. Ranged right text (also known as ragged left) is used less frequently than text ranged left (ragged right), or justified. The ragged left-hand margin does make it harder for the reader to follow the text.

56 characters per line (12 words)

37 characters per line (6 words)

10 characters per line (12 words)

ine is too long to read all at once

if there were more lines, and if
n tight linespacing that the words

T h e
m e a -
s u r e
f o r
t h i s
text is
t o o
n a r -
row.

If the measure is too short the result will be either bad word breaks (if you hyphenate) or lines consisting of only one word (if you don't hyphenate).

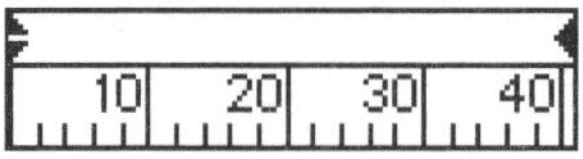

This caption is set in Futura, which is a fairly wide-bodied font. Because of this, not many words will fit on a narrow measure, resulting in bad wordbreaks.

This caption is set in Helvetica Condensed, a narrow-bodied font suitable for setting type across narrow measures.

If you need to use a short measure, pick a narrow-bodied or condensed typeface which will allow more characters per line and so reduce word breaks. Picture captions, which are often set across tiny measures, work best in small sizes and condensed type.

3/6 *Emphasis*

DIFFERENT versions of a typeface can be used to add impact to particular words or to reduce the amount of punctuation needed. Gossip columns often make bold with people's names. Italics are pressed into action for book and film names, to minimise the number of intrusive punctuation marks. Setting quotes around every instance would be far too ugly.

Changing your body face like this can add a lot of 'colour' to your copy, enticing the casual reader to read on from a bold word that may have caught **her** eye...

SETTING A LAR
TEXT IN CAPITA
SERIOUSLY
LEGIBILITY OF

Different versions of a typeface can be used to add impact to particular words or to reduce the amount of punctuation needed. Gossip columns often make **bold** with people's **names.** Italics are pressed into action for book and film names, to minimise the number of intrusive punctuation marks.

Picking out a word in bold is a **common** way of adding emphasis.

Italics are used for quotations, and to *add* extra, *subtle* emphasis.

If you MUST use capitals for EMPHASIS, remember to set them a little SMALLER than the surrounding text.

If you're using capitals for emphasis, it is worth opening up the letter spacing slightly, otherwise the copy looks unevenly dark.

If you use the 'small caps' option in the type styles menu, the computer simply scales down the capitals, and the stem width changes.
Expert sets of fonts, eg Adobe Garamond, contain true small capitals which have the same weight as capitals and lowercase characters.

GE AMOUNT OF
LETTERS WILL
IMPAIR THE
THE PASSAGE

For real emphasis, words can be reversed out of the background.

Reversing out a single word can have huge impact but beware entanglements with ascenders and descenders from the surrounding lines.

Underlining a word is a hangover from typewriter days, and should be avoided.

DTP makes setting tables a whole lot easier. Dividing boxes into equally sized rows and columns is all taken care of for you, and it's easy to experiment with different formats for information, whether it's deciding to centre or range left the figures, or to highlight a single row in red.

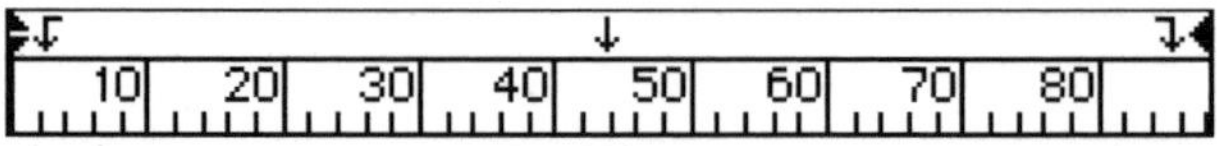

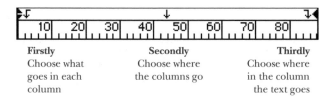

Firstly	Secondly	Thirdly
Choose what goes in each column	Choose where the columns go	Choose where in the column the text goes

Numbers and text in tables can be arranged in many different ways. While words read best ranged left at the left and centred in central columns, numbers make more sense centred around the decimal point, so that it becomes easier for the reader to spot different values.

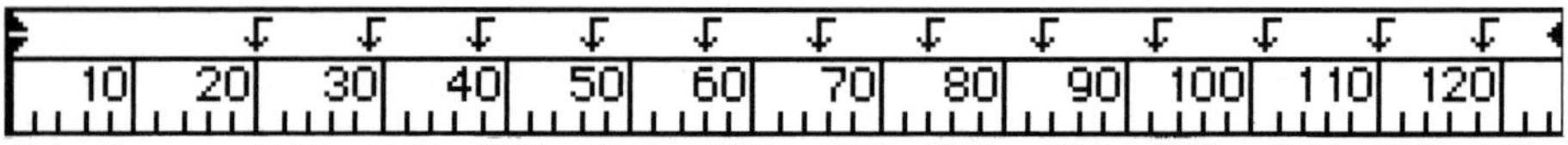

Alphaville	1123	*1156*	1207	*1219*	1227	*1245*	1302	*1311*	1319	*1327*	1343	*1351*
Beta-Block	1143	*1217*	1228	*1240*	1248	*1306*	1323	*1332*	1340	*1348*	1404	*1412*
Gammatown	1153	*1227*	1238	*1250*	1258	*1316*	1333	*1342*	1350	*1358*	1414	*1422*
Deltic arr.	1200	*1234*	1245	*1257*	1305	*1323*	1340	*1349*	1357	*1355*	1421	*1429*
dep.	**1203**	***1237***	**1248**	***1300***	**1308**	***1326***	**1343**	***1352***	**1400**	***1408***	**1424**	***1432***
Epitome	1248	*1300*	1308	*1326*	1343	*1352*	1400	*1408*	1424	*1432*	1446	*1456*
Pheromone City	1343	*1417*	1428	*1440*	1448	*1506*	1523	*1532*	1540	*1548*	1604	*1612*

If you have a great deal of numbers in a table, it is a good idea to emphasise alternate columns. You can do this typographically by making columns italic or bold, or by filling the background of some columns or columns with tint.

Decimal tabs align the text such that the decimal point stays under the tab marker. Numerals are almost always non-proportionately spaced; this makes for tidier setting of columns of figures where all the tens, hundreds and thousands need to be in the same position to add up properly.

£5,348,234.00
£5,221.00
£673.56
£56.32
£0.78
£0.0023
£5354185.6623

Wedding Present	Christina & William	Pat & Roger	Iris & Aladar
Mask	Moof	Jimmy	☺☺
Whisk	Cantor	Elvis	☺☺☺
Feint	Kawasaki	George	☺
Jimmy	Bowls	Neal	☺
Poem	Neck	Chris	☺☺☺
Dave the Rave	Lights	KLF	☺

When setting tables don't just rely on your DTP package. Business-oriented word processing packages and spreadsheets often offer superior facilities for setting simple tables: for example, Microsoft Word 4.0 allows the figures in one column to be highlighted, not possible in contemporary Mac DTP software.

To help the reader trace across columns, it is conventional to use tab leaders (usually dots or dashes). Most DTP applications allow you to choose what kind of tab leader to use.

●●●●●●●●●●●●●●●●●●●●●●.dotty

■■■■■■■■■■■■■■ Square

FF 96.053,02

£96,053.02

Conventions for breaking up large numbers differ from country to country; in France a comma replaces the decimal point, and the full point marks off thousands.

THE END

Director	Alex Gollner
Producer	David Collier
Story	David Collier
Screenplay	Carol Atack
Second Unit Director	Lynn Clark
Best Boy	Nick Franchini
Gaffer	Paul Khera

Decimal tabs can be used to create credits – make the full-stops the same colour as the background.

4 Pun;ctuation

GOOD punctuation should be invisible to the reader, carefully guiding him through the text and making sense of complicated sentences. That is its sole purpose, and remembering this simple rule should make dealing with punctuation easier. If a punctuation mark screams out of the text, it's almost certainly incorrect and shouldn't be there. Excessive use of punctuation marks breaks up the flow of the text and may make the words harder rather than easier to read.

While attempts have been made to write up precise rules for punctuation, english is a living language and punctuation is part of its evolutionary process. Fashions and conventions change over the years; the ancient Greeks used no punctuation at all, nineteenth century English typesetting was a riot of typographical excess, and some modern writers have attempted to free themselves from tyranny by using no or very limited punctuation. Good punctuation is mainly a matter of observing contemporary custom and practice and then following it. You may get complaints from some pedantic readers but you shouldn't make too many gross errors.

DTP applications make punctuation simpler to deal with as consistent errors in text can be rooted out and corrected with search and replace functions. This also applies to typographical fine tuning which is needed when turning word-processed text, or typewritten text which has been scanned into the computer, into well-set type.

A constant offender is the hyphen, used where there should be an em rule. On old-fashioned typewriters it was possible to indicate that an em rule was required by typing two hyphens with no space in between them. This neatly created the longer em rule. However, on most word processors typing two hyphens creates exactly that – two hyphens separated by a small gap – on screen and in the printout, so many writers simply type a single hyphen when they want an em rule. In fact, on the Macintosh most word-processing programs will produce an en rule by pressing the option key when typing a hyphen, and a longer em rule by pressing the shift and option keys when typing a hyphen. Most DTP applications can pick up single or double hyphens and replace them with em or en rules automatically.

Typists make two spaces after a full point before beginning the next sentence. This looks horrible when typeset, so always search for and replace any double spaces.

Quotation marks are where the punctuation war really begins. There are several choices to make here: single or double quotes, curly quotes or inch and foot marks, and so on. Double curly quotes are the style you were probably taught to write at school, but in newspapers and similar documents with many brief quotations, double quotes can look obtrusive. They look especially bad at the beginning of paragraphs. Single quotes are therefore better in this type of document, but where quoted speech is infrequent, double quotes can be considered. Two points to remember: if the quote runs on for more than a paragraph use a new set of opening quotes at the beginning of each paragraph, and whether you're using double or single quotes use the other kind for quotes within quotes.

The battle between curly quotes and inch marks continues to rage. Inch marks used to be the sign of the typewriter, and early word processors. Now DTP programs are capable of replacing inch marks with correctly-sexed curly quotes. Curly quotes are probably preferable for body copy, where they are what the reader is expecting. But for pull quotes, or for any quotes which stand out from the main body of text, inch marks may be more suitable. They may fit the context better, and will almost certainly be more appropriate if you are using a modern, highly-condensed typeface. This is even more true if the face has a deliberate computer-generated look. In such cases, the quotation marks serve more as a graphic device than as punctuation. Be careful with punctuation around the quotes. As a quick rule of thumb, English style is to keep punctuation with the part of the sentence to which it belongs.

Fnally, a word on punctuating headings and captions. If at all possible, don't. The marks detract from the impact of the large letters. Headings and captions should be strong and simple enough in their expression not to need punctuating. The exception is the colon, which is used to indicate the subject of a picture, or the main theme of a long running story; for example 'AIDS: miracle cure'.

4/1 Punctuation symbols

Q. What's the dfference between a tiger and a sentence ?

PUNCTUATION is full of pitfalls which can leave your text looking rather messy and your readers confused. Simplicity and consistency are the keys to success; if the copy needs a lot of punctuation it probably also needs rewriting to help it make sense. Define a house style and keep to it, deciding when to use commas, and when dashes or brackets would be more appropriate. Try to match all use of punctuation to this style.

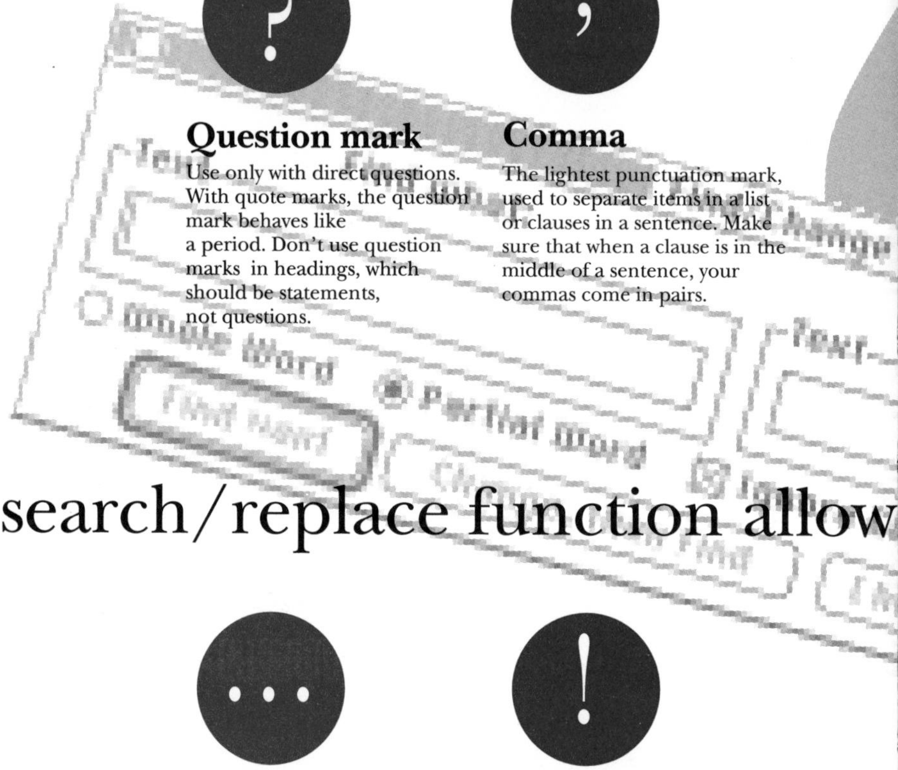

Question mark

Use only with direct questions. With quote marks, the question mark behaves like a period. Don't use question marks in headings, which should be statements, not questions.

Comma

The lightest punctuation mark, used to separate items in a list or clauses in a sentence. Make sure that when a clause is in the middle of a sentence, your commas come in pairs.

The search/replace function allow

Ellipsis points

This set of three full points indicates omissions from quoted material. Leave spaces around them when they show a gap in the middle of a sentence. Use with no preceding space at the end of an item in less formal text…

Exclamation mark

Known in typesetting as a screamer, it should only be used in reported speech after exclamations and at the end of sentences, never to add emphasis and never in headlines.

Hyphen

Used to join two words together, or to indicate where a word has been broken over two lines. Never confuse with the dash or em rule.

Dash

Used in pairs – often instead of brackets – to enclose a parenthetic or subsidiary thought. Use sparingly and don't confuse with the much-abused hyphen. *Collier's Rules* suggests leaving a space on either side of the dash.

Long dash

Also called the em-dash or mutt-rule, some typographers prefer to use it instead of an en dash—like this with no surrounding space—but notice the big holes this produces in the text. Also used to bridge dates.

Beware of confusing your punctuation symbols – dashes are one thing – hyphen-ation is another.

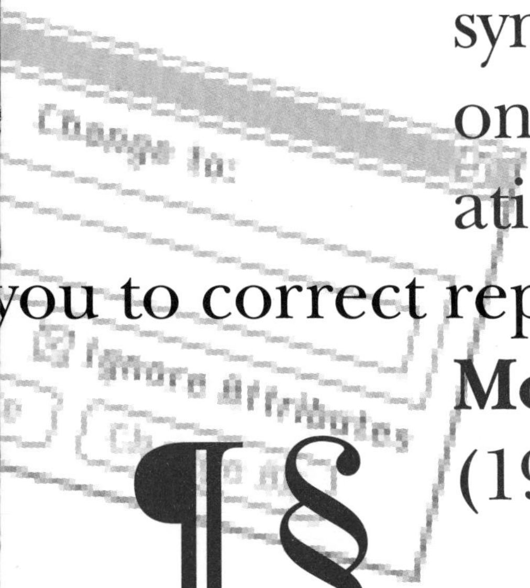

you to correct repetitive errors fast

Mouse, Michael M. (1926—94)

¶§

Paragraph Mark & Section Mark. Can be used to show new paras or sections, or used to refer to other sections or paragraphs in the book.

More punctuation coming soon…

A. One has paws at the end of its claws, the other has a pause at the end of its clause.

9:50am

A GOOD punctuation style should mean that the punctuation isn't obvious to the reader. Guided through sentences by colons, commas and parentheses, the reader will not have to struggle to make sense of the text. Too much punctuation has the opposite effect, breaking up the flow of the sense of the words.

The simplest forms of punctuation are usually the best; use plain brackets rather than curly or square brackets. These latter should never really stray beyond the pages of technical literature and maths text books.

Parentheses

These are used to separate a clause attached to a particular word in a sentence. Use carefully and sparingly as they can become confusing. For parentheses within parentheses use curly or square brackets, if there's no avoiding such a complex sentence.

(

A parenth

(Use brackets for a {parent

Period

The full point or period marks the end of a sentence, except when ? or ! are used to denote questions or exclamations. When a full sentence is quoted, the period goes with the sentence inside the quote marks.

Henry VIII Don't use a period with roma

.

A period e

Colon

Used to indicate the other half of a thought equation, or a related but contradictory thought. Sometimes used to precede quoted speech. Never follow with a dash.

:

Don't use a

Colons follow the salutation in formal corresponden

Semi-colon

Semi-colons separate two parts of a sentence which are distinct thoughts but nonetheless in agreement with each other. They are a little old-fashioned, but useful in complex text. Sometimes a sentence contains two parts; a semi-colon is then appropriate.

;

This is a s

Some applications; namely,

$$[\{P_0 + 2P_1 + P_2\} - \{P_6 + 2P_2 + P_6\}]^2$$

Use square and curly brackets in mathematical and scientific contexts.

ical clause in parentheses

cal expression} within parentheses.)

umerals, whether capitals or lower-case,

ds the sentence.

unless the numeral is being used to list a number of headings or points, eg I. Punctuation problems.

colon like this :-

To whom it may concern:

mi-colon;

Illustrator, Quark XPress…

THESE are potentially the most intrusive punctuation marks and also an area where publishing whims abound – single or double sets, 'smart quotes' or unsexed inch marks. Controlling all these options in standard DTP programs is often quite tricky as the computer insists that once you've chosen curly double quotes, you'll have to hunt hard to produce straight up and down inch marks.

“This is a 'sin

'single quotes are less “intru

"These are inch

He said “I thought you'd ask, man.” *(USA style)*

“These are cur

He said “I thought you'd ask, old boy”. *(UK style)*

«Mots entre gu

Different styles of opening quotes

„Anführung

Although most typefaces don't have quotation mark styles for each different convention, you can create your own alternatives.

“Hanging punctuation can enhance
visual appearances,” said Alex.
“Otherwise the effect produced can
look somewhat ragged, like this”.

e quote’

” than double quotes’

‘ ’

Single quotes work best in body text as they break up the type less. Never use quotes to pick out words or names; it’s far too precious when italic type can do the job with less disruption to the text and more impact. Quotes within quotes need to be differentiated.

narks"

" "

Inch marks for speech were the hall-mark of unsophisticated DTP output. But they can make a statement – putting neat curly quotes around deliberately bitmapped jaggy type will ruin its impact.

quotes”

“ ”

Double quotation marks can be intrusive in body text but offer more graphic impact when used for pull quotes. American and english have different conventions for punctuation around quotations. Kerning is advised wherever a full-stop meets a quotation mark.

llemets»

« »

European languages each have their own conventions for punctuating speech. French ‘guillemets’ have a character all of their own.

eichen“

„ “

Note that German speech punctuation differs slightly from the English convention. It would work well for pull quotes in a suitably themed article.

Don’t confuse the mid 1830s with the ’thirties or even the ’30s

4/4 Accents & rights

FORTUNATELY for Macintosh users, most typefaces implement special characters in a standard way. Access them with the option key; if you can't remember where to find a particular character, the Key Caps desk accessory, installed on every Mac under the Apple menu, maps out all the characters available in the system font, although not every typeface will have all of these.

Accents are easily added with an option key plus letter combination typed before the letter you want to accent. This is called overstrike. Most work with all vowels in both capitals and upper-case, although some marks will only work with letters which the Mac believes are appropriate.

é

Option 'e'. This is an example of the overstrike theory, in this case producing an acute accent. Hold down the option key and type 'e', then type 'e' again to produce the character, eg *en êté.*

è

Option '`' 'e' produces an 'e' with a grave accent, in the same way, eg *grève.*

ç

Option 'c' produces a cedilla. Hold down the option key and type 'c', eg *français.*

Option 'u' produces an umlaut over a following a, o or u, eg *Göttingen.*

ü

Option 's' produces the German double s, eg *straße.*

ß

Option 'i' produces a circumflex over vowels, eg *rôle.*

î

õ

Shift option 'm' produces a tilde which can be kerned on to the appropriate letter; option 'n' produces a slightly larger tilde which appears over n, o, and a, and before other letters.

ı

Option 'k' and shift-option-'b' produce a dot and a dotless i respectively, to use with accented letters in languages such as Turkish.

Ê

Most accented capital vowels can be produced more easily by using shift-option which maps many of these letters on to the keyboard, eg Ê is produced by shift-option-t.

© ® ℗

Option 'g' produces a copyright symbol in most typefaces.

Option 'a' creates this symbol, which is a unit of measurement.

Å

TM

™ indicates that a logo is a trademark. The symbol is accessed through option '2', but you can create your own and use baseline shift or superscript for positioning.

This is the symbol by which record companies indicate the ownership of a sound recording. Unfortunately there is no direct keyboard equivalent; the simplest solution is to alter the ® symbol (option 'r') using an application such as FontStudio.

SYMBOLS and signs for mathematical use also appear on the Macintosh keyboard through the option key. Most of the Greek letters used in maths and science can be accessed this way, but to produce good looking equations and formulæ it may be better to use a special equation-setting program. However, some DTP applications (such as FrameMaker), which are designed for technical publishing, include modules for setting equations.

Footnotes can be indicated with either symbols or superscript numbers or letters. Symbols are better for occasional notes; documents with several footnotes, such as academic papers, should be referenced with numbered footnotes.

The majority of typefaces have currency symbols; use Key Caps to find out where they are on the keyboard. Illustrated here are: florin, yen, international currency symbol, dollar, cent, pound.

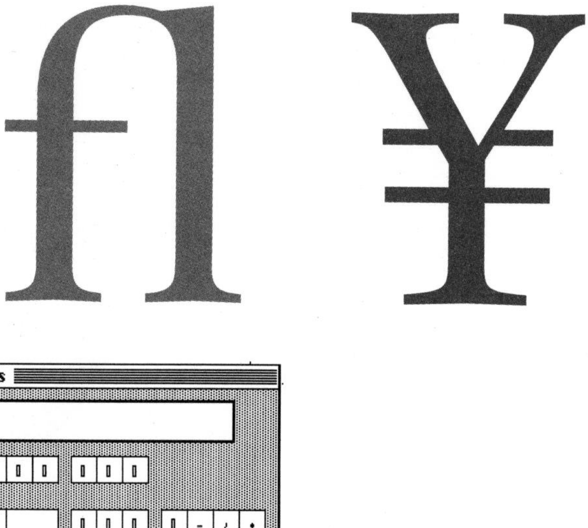

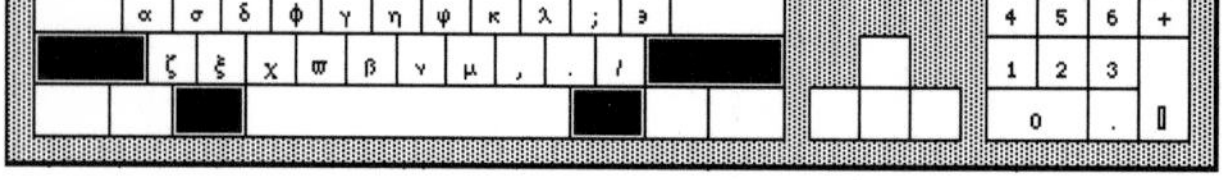

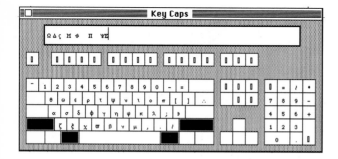

Greek letters for science and statistics are found both in the symbol font and with the option key. However, if you're setting actual Greek language text, you may want to investigate a more modern Greek typeface. Other mathematical symbols such as infinity (∞ is produced by option'5') are dotted around the keyboard – check using Key Caps.

mediæval

phœnix

Some words still use diphthongs, two vowels joined together, and these are accessible through the option key. Examples are option'q' for œ, and option'-' for æ. However, dipthongs can look peculiarly old-fashioned in modern and sans serif faces and are probably best reserved for serif faces.

∞ ¤ $ ¢ £

Find Superscript and Subscript in the type styles menu

$< \; > \; \cong \; \leq$

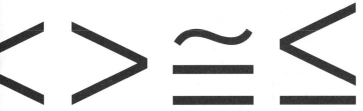

Mathematical signs for logical statements (used in symbolic logic) can also be found on the keyboard and are supported by most typefaces.

5 Paragraphs

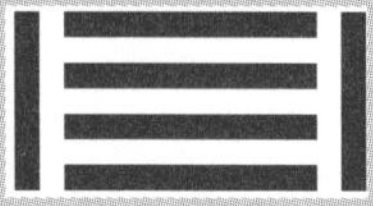

THE SHAPE of each paragraph on the page can make a huge difference to the overall look of a document; after the choice of typeface it probably has the most influence on the colour of the page, and how inviting it looks to the reader. To start with, the length of paragraphs can attract or turn off the reader; a paragraph is supposed to express a single, self-contained stage in the story or argument, so the longer the paragraph, the more complicated the text will seem to the reader.

Short paragraphs are therefore best for shorter, newsy texts, while longer pieces meant for continuous reading can contain larger paragraphs because the reader becomes more involved with the text and does not need it to be presented in pre-digested chunks.

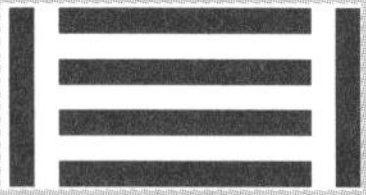

However, length is only one dimension of the paragraph's shape. The smoothness or otherwise of its outline is another important factor. Text can be justified, so that both right and left edge are straight, or ranged left or right so that only one edge is straight and the other is jagged according to the differing lengths of lines.

Each approach has its merits and uses; justified text is more economical of space and generally better for documents where columns of text are the key element on each page, such as newspapers. Text ranged left is easier to read, because words are usually not hyphenated and there is less letter spacing, but the jagged edge of the text can look strange if it abuts the smooth edge of the next column. Ranged left or ragged right, as it is sometimes known, works better where text and graphics have equal prominence on a page, or short text items are scattered around, for example in pictorial spreads in teenage magazines.

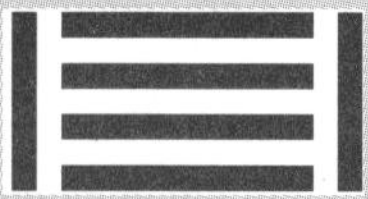

Ranged-right or ragged-left text is difficult to read for more than a few lines at a time because it is hard for the reader to find the beginning of the next line. It works best where text has to be aligned to a graphic or picture to caption it; here it stands out well from other text items on the same page. Of course all three styles can be used together to highlight particular paragraphs or make stories stand out from each other; the trick is to create a range of text styles and to stick to it for consistency.

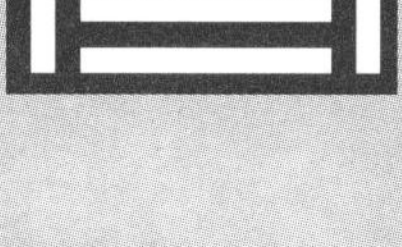

Justified text introduces one of the necessary evils of typesetting; hyphenation. Breaking words across lines saves a lot of space, and in justified text reduces excessive letter and word spacing to a readable minimum. All DTP programs include a hyphenation dictionary so that they can carry out this task automatically; in the old hot-metal days it was the compositor's job to decide when to hyphenate and when to word and letter space. Hyphenation in DTP varies in sophistication and it is always worth reading text carefully to check that there are no bad word breaks which would make it hard for the reader to understand what is going on, or simply make sure that every line in a column is not hyphenated, which usually looks pretty awful and suggests some rewriting or over-riding of the program's automatic hyphenation. Another problem to watch for is the creation of rude and inappropriate words by inopportune word breaks; while programs will probably avoid such examples as the-rapist, they will often do terrible things to proper names which their dictionary doesn't know about. Another thing to check is that any hyphens created by the hyphenation process disappear when the text is reflowed, which sometimes fails to happen.

Hyphenation works by holding a dictionary which lists all the possible places to break a word, and categorises these according to their desirability. When you hyphenate a text you will be able to select the level of hyphenation you want, and only the types of word breaks you have specified will be used. Where there is no good break and no other way of tidying up the line by altering spacing, high-end software will show this problem by allowing the word to stick out past the edge of the line, so that you can spot it easily and sort out the problem by rewriting or allowing an extra level of hyphenation which may produce a satisfactory word break. However, most DTP software will simply make the best break possible, which often isn't good enough. Rewriting is the best solution.

Breaks in paragraphs themselves need to be watched for. If a paragraph straddles two columns, make sure that its first and last lines do not begin or end a column, as this breaks up the shape of the column. Short single-word or syllable lines at the ends of paragraphs are known as widows and should be avoided; where they occur at the top of a column they are known as orphans and even more effort should be paid to filling out the line. Some DTP programs will do this for you but at the expense of good word and letter spacing; it's probably better to take care of this manually. Crossheads and other text breakers should also be placed at the beginning of paragraphs, and the next paragraph should not be indented.

DIFFERENT arrangements of text each work well in different contexts. Ranged left (or ragged right as it is sometimes called) works best with simple text without hyphenation. Its opposite, ranged right, is less useful as it is hard for readers to find the next line; it's most useful for picture captions where the caption needs to be visually attached to the text. Centred text is best for text not meant to be read as a whole – menus, lists, lyrics and poetry – and needs plenty of space. Justified text, where both edges are firm, is best for designs heavy in text. Hyphenation is needed to keep gaps between words down to an acceptable minimum.

R/L

In cybernetics, entropy is generalised to measure the tendency of any system to move from a less to a more probable state, using the same mathematical apparatus as physics.

R/R

In cybernetics, entropy is generalised to measure the tendency of any system to move from a less to a more probable state, using the same mathematical apparatus as physics.

---

ctr.

In cybernetics, entropy is generalised to measure the tendency of any system to move from a less to a more probable state, using the same mathematical apparatus as physics.

---

just.

In cybernetics, entropy is generalised to measure the tendency of any system to move from a less to a more probable state, using the same mathematical apparatus as physics.

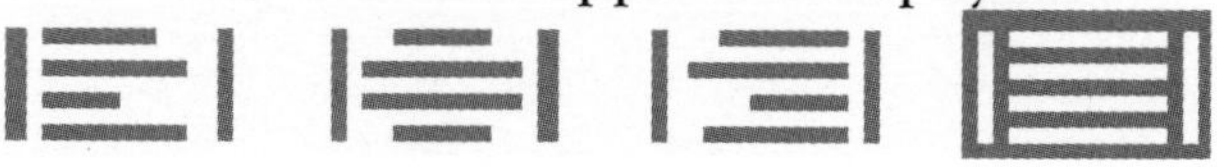

Distinct passage or section in book etc. usually marked by indentation of first line; symbol formerly used to mark new paragraph, now as reference mark.

Hence **paragraphic** – write paragraph about (person, thing); arrange in paragraph. [from the Greek *graphos* short stroke marking break in sense].

Distinct passage or section in book etc. usually marked by indentation of first line; symbol formerly used to mark new paragraph, now as reference mark.

Hence **paragraphic** – write paragraph about (person, thing); arrange in paragraph. [from the Greek *graphos* short stroke marking break in sense].

Paragraphs present text in digestible mouthfuls. There are several conventions for representing them; the most used is to indent the first line by an em, but bullets, line spaces, the old paragraph mark and indenting the whole paragraph provide variety.

Context is the key, and the text should provide clues to the most suitable style. Bullets work well for a group of short single paragraph items, but would unduly disrupt the flow of a magazine feature.

Distinct passage or section in book etc. usually marked by indentation of first line; symbol formerly used to mark new paragraph, now as reference mark.

Hence paragraphic – write paragraph about (person, thing); arrange in paragraph. [from the Greek *graphos* short stroke marking break in sense].

- Distinct passage or section in book etc. usually marked by indentation of first line; symbol formerly used to mark new paragraph, now as reference mark.
- Hence **paragraphic** – write paragraph about (person, thing); arrange in paragraph. [from the Greek *graphos* short stroke marking break in sense].

Distinct passage or section in book etc. usually marked by indentation of first line; symbol formerly used to mark new paragraph, now as reference mark.

Hence **paragraphic** – write paragraph about (person, thing); arrange in paragraph.

From the Greek *graphos* short stroke marking break in sense.

Distinct passage or section in book etc. usually marked by indentation of first line; symbol formerly used to mark new paragraph, now as reference mark. ¶ Hence **paragraphic** – write paragraph about (person, thing); arrange in paragraph. [from the Greek *graphos* short stroke marking break in sense].

5/2 Leading

THE SPACE between lines is important both for readability and the overall look of the page. Too much and lines can float off; too little and the text becomes too dense to read comfortably. Computers make it possible to experiment with different values of leading, and try things which were impossible in the days of hot metal, when leading was exactly that – strips of lead inserted between the lines of type. Now the trend is to use a point or two of leading all the time.

negative leadin
was never po
with hot m
who real

The space between lines is important both for readability and the overall look of the page. Too much and lines can float off; too little and the text becomes far too dense to read comfortably.

Computers make it possible to experiment with different values of leading, and try things that were impossible in the days of hot metal.

The space between lines is important both for readability and the overall look of the page. Too much and lines can float off; too little and the text becomes far too dense to read comfortably.

Computers make it possible to experiment with different values of leading, and try things that were impossible in the days of hot metal.

Word processing software distributes the leading below the ascenders of the type. If the type size increases on a line, the extra space afforded by the larger ascender is ignored; the type is set too low, the leading having been measured from the ascender of the larger type downwards.

Typesetting software calculates leading from baseline to baseline. At first glance, the lines appear to be equally spaced.

The space between lines is important both for readability and the overall look of the page. Too much and lines can float off; too little and the text becomes too dense to read comfortably.

Computers make it possible to experiment with different values of leading, and try things which were impossible in the days of hot metal, when leading was exactly that – strips of lead inserted between lines of type.

The space between lines is important both for readability and the overall look of the page. Too much and lines can float off; too little and the text becomes too dense to read comfortably.

Computers make it possible to experiment with different values of leading, and try things which were impossible in the days of hot metal, when leading was exactly that – strips of lead inserted between lines of type.

Most typefaces have an automatic leading value attached to each type size. This will not necessarily be the same for each font, as these examples of eight point Futura and Helvetica show. If you are using more than one typeface, set the leading yourself to ensure consistency.

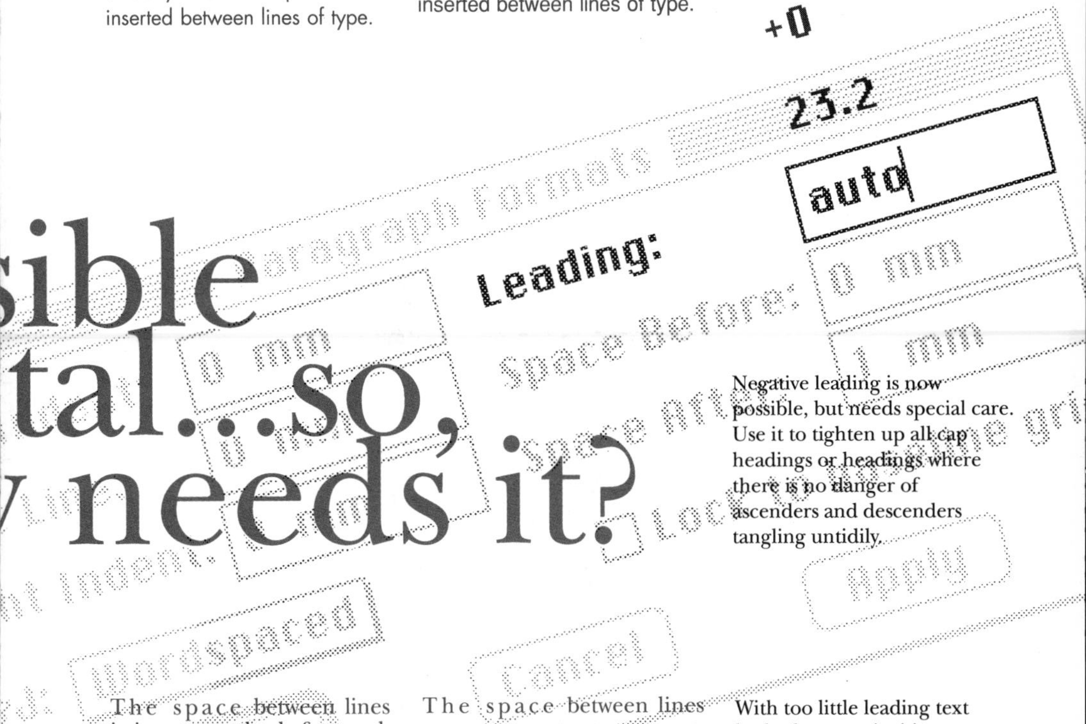

Negative leading is now possible, but needs special care. Use it to tighten up all-cap headings or headings where there is no danger of ascenders and descenders tangling untidily.

The space between lines is important both for readability and the overall look of the page. Too much and lines can float off; too little and the text becomes too dense to read comfortably.

Computers make it possible to experiment with different values of leading, and try things which were impossible in the days of hot metal, when leading was exactly that – strips of lead inserted between the lines of type.

The space between lines is important both for readability and the overall look of the page. Too much and lines can float off; too little and the text becomes too dense to read comfortably.

Computers make it possible to experiment with different values of leading, and try things which were impossible in the days of hot metal, when leading was exactly that – strips of lead inserted between the lines of type.

With too little leading text looks dense, uninviting and old-fashioned. A couple of points leading makes text much easier on the modern eye.

JUSTIFICATION creates a neat edge to the column of text, at some cost to the letter and word spacing within it. How much extra space you will allow before you resort to hyphenation needs to be clearly thought out; your aim should be to maintain the colour of the type and not to stretch words and letters so much that they become hard to read, or to squash them up so much that the page becomes black. Other problems of spacing include widows and orphans which also break up the shape of the column and the flow of the text and need to be edited out.

Widows are single lines of text left alone at the tops of columns. Orphans are lines of text left over from paragraphs at the bottom of columns, and single words left as the last lines of paragraphs. Both can be avoided by scrupulous copy editing, or bringing a word around from a previous line.

Once upon a time, Lynn, the PANTONE™ fairy, was colouring the world in coated reflex blue, warm red and uncoated P361. Paul, the shy and ebullient elf, wrestled with a particularly mean and ornery business letterhead while David was having a heart to heart with an old confidante...

He went on, stuttering, "Yes, Widow Harding,

To justify type, the computer adds extra space between words and letters to create a neat right-hand edge. The first paragraph shows all the space distributed between the letters (letter spaced), followed by a paragraph with the space between the words (word spaced), then 50% wordspacing and 50% letterspacing.

The spacing is still poor, so allowing hyphenation gives the computer more options in fitting the lines.

The second column shows hyphenation; firstly a paragraph with automatic hyphenation and then a paragraph with manual hyphenation.

Letter spaced

Hyphens in a book are a necessary evil. Readers often notice them far less than they would notice massively stretched letter & word spaces.

Word spaced

Hyphens in a book are a necessary evil. Readers often notice them far less than they would notice massively stretched letter & word spaces.

Letter & word spaced

Hyphens in a book are a necessary evil. Readers often notice them far less than they would notice massively stretched letter & word spaces.

Automatic Hyphenation

Hyphens in a book are a neces-sary evil. Readers often notice them far less than they would notice massively stretched letter & word spaces.

Manual Hyphenation

Hyphens in a book are a necess-ary evil. Readers often notice them far less than they would notice massively stretched letter & word spaces.

Justify

Spreading Out

A 'soft return' at the end of a line forces the last words to spread across the measure.

Use a flush zone to simplify justification. It is measured from the right-hand edge of the measure. If the last word ends within the zone, the last line will be spread across the measure. To distribute the space equally, use non-breaking spaces between the last words.

Please fill the lines from beginning to end.

Please fill the lines from beginning to end.

Please fill the lines from beginning to end.

I am an orphan..."

"Don't worry dear," she said, "you're only an example in a book of typographic rules"

"Oh, that's alright then!" he beamed, and they both went skipping through the clauses, and çedillas until it was time for a huge slap-up tea!

THE END

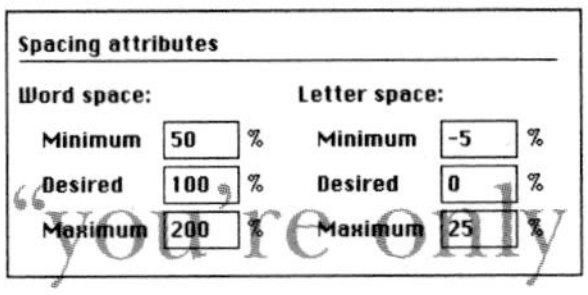

Crucial to quality setting is the technique used to expand the text to make it justify to the measure. Most DTP programs allow fine control to select whether spacing should be changed between characters or letters in order to fit a line.

The 'minimum' distance is how much the computer can condense spaces to squash words into a line. The 'maximum' value is the amount the computer can expand each space to fill out a line.

It is neccesary to have space between words, so expanding these spaces is less noticeable than adding space between lettters. It is a matter of personal preference, but *Collier's Rules* recommends not adding letter spacing.

Optimum values need to be carefully checked against bromide proofs. Some fonts seem very open, that is they contain much internal spacing. If you are setting magazines with tight leading, the reader's eye may skip to the next line if the gap between words is bigger than the linespacing. As *Collier's Rules* has generous leading, the optimum word spaces were opened up slightly.

Spacing and hyphenation look good in justified text when you get the balance between typeface, size and measure right.

8pt New Baskerville

Hyphens in a book are a necessary evil. Readers often notice them far less than they would notice stretched letter & word spaces.

7pt Franklin Gothic

Hyphens in a book are a necessary evil. Readers often notice them far less than they would notice massively stretched letter & word spaces.

8pt Bembo

Hyphens in a book are a necessary evil. Readers often notice them far less than they would notice massively stretched letter & word spaces.

8pt Garamond

Hyphens in a book are a necessary evil. Readers often notice them far less than they would notice massively stretched letter & word spaces.

8pt Futura Book

Hyphens in a book are a necessary evil. Readers often notice them far less than they would notice massively stretched letter & word spaces.

8pt Futura Light

Hyphens in a book are a necessary evil. Readers often notice them far less than they would notice massively stretched letter & word spaces.

Mac-in-tosh

Page-Maker

Write-Now

Hyper-Card

Mac-Draw

BREAKING up is hard to do, especially where words are concerned. Hyphenation algorithms are some of the most important features of DTP programs, and the most difficult to implement; the computer's dictionary needs to know where each word in the language can be broken and where the best break – the one which is easiest for readers to understand – is to be found. Sometimes hyphenation is impossible, and then some systems will leave a word sticking out for sub-editors to sort out.

On most DTP systems it's advisable to check for bad word-breaks and rewrite if necessary, or experiment with word and letter spacing to avoid hyphenation. Another gremlin to watch out for is redundant hyphens staying in the text after it has been reflowed on to the page.

Graveolent

Gra-veolent

Grav-eolent

Grave-olent

Graveo-lent

Does the word have three syllables or four? Is the break between the e and o allowed?

As it is pronounced gra-ve-o-lent, it's ok to hyphenate it that way.

Hyphenation Method

1	B	C	D	F	G	M	N	P	R	T	V	X
2	B	C	D	F	J	M	N	P	S	T	V	W
3	B	C	D	F	M	N	P	T	V	Z		
4	K	H										

Hyphenate when group 1 characters are followed by group 2, and when characters in group 3 are followed by characters in group 4.

Check how the computer will hyphenate using this chart and teach programs any special names or words it should take care with.

You can create your own list of hyphenation exceptions; words that will not be hyphenated correctly by the method above. The list can be used in conjunction with your personal dictionary to make glossaries and indices for the documents that you create using a specialised set of words.

Dis-[4]-com-[3]-bob-[1]-u-[2]-lation

big fat shouted

Sophisticated hyphenation systems, such as that on PageMaker and Atex, have several hyphenation levels, starting with the best break for each word listed and moving along to less and less desirable breaks. When hyphenating, you can choose which levels you are prepared to accept.

Watch out for word breaks which result in a rude or inappropriate word being formed on one line.

at? Arse-

bottom of

football

ue?"

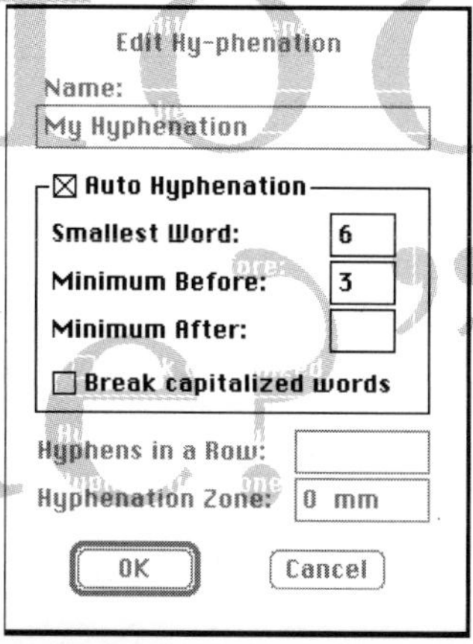

Hyphenation usually includes several options; this dialog box allows you to set minimum word length for hyphenation, and letters before and after the line break. It also allows you to keep proper names all on one line and to prevent hyphens occurring on every line, and it stipulates how close to the edge of the line a word should be to be eligible for hyphenation.

This is an example of hyphenated multisyllable paragraphs. Hyphenation dialogs control the number of consecutive hyphens.

This is an example of hyphenated multisyllable paragraphs. Hyphenation dialogs control the number of consecutive hyphens.

6 Illustrations & graphics

ONE of the delights of desktop design is that it makes it so much easier to combine text and images. Not only do DTP programs make it easy to place the two in the same document and experiment till you get it right, but a whole range of graphics applications allow you to create highly finished images more quickly than you could have done before, allowing you to experiment in ways which would previously have been technically impossible. There are plenty of cheats and tricks of the trade to discover; many a marbled background began life as a crumpled sheet of paper scanned into an image manipulation package. If all you have to work with is an unflattering black and white photo of a less than handsome subject, adding false colour can improve the image almost beyond recognition.

Scanned images are only one source of ideas. Apart from creating your own drawings using painting or drawing packages, you also have access to a wide range of ready to use graphics, known as clip art. Unfortunately the vast majority of these are not very high quality, and you need to watch out for copyright problems as computers make it very easy to steal images. You don't want an aggrieved illustrator turning up in your studio demanding a reproduction fee and blowing your budget.

The illustration world is divided into two hemispheres, object-oriented drawing packages which treat images as lines, points and proportions and consequently handle them more intelligently, and bitmap painting packages where an image is just a collection of pixels. When you scan a picture or logo into your computer it will be a bitmap, but you can use a tracing package such as Adobe Streamline to convert it into a PostScript file. This is particularly useful for logos and similar graphics where you may want to resize your scanned original but want to remain faithful to it. The tracing is automatic but you can go over it by hand to add extra points along curves to improve the quality.

Another set of differences you will have to come to terms with is the wide range of graphics formats. Several have evolved over the years, from the original MacPaint for simple mono illustrations to 24-bit versions of TIFF and PICT, the two main competitors, which support the latest true colour images. It's a good idea to standardise on one format for any particular venture, as this makes it easier for whoever is handling the final output. Even if images make it on to the page as encapsulated PostScript files, it's a good idea to send a non-PostScript original to the bureau in case problems are encountered. In fact the choice of file format is probably best made by the experts at the bureau as different formats take different lengths of time to output on imagesetters. While this is often unpredictable, it may be that the work you do comes out quicker in TIFF and it will save you money and bureau time by sticking to that standard. Settling on a standard also means you will have fewer difficulties with work by freelance illustrators being incompatible with your software. So choosing a standard is a good idea but which standard to choose is probably best discovered by the experience of your studio and the type of work you do.

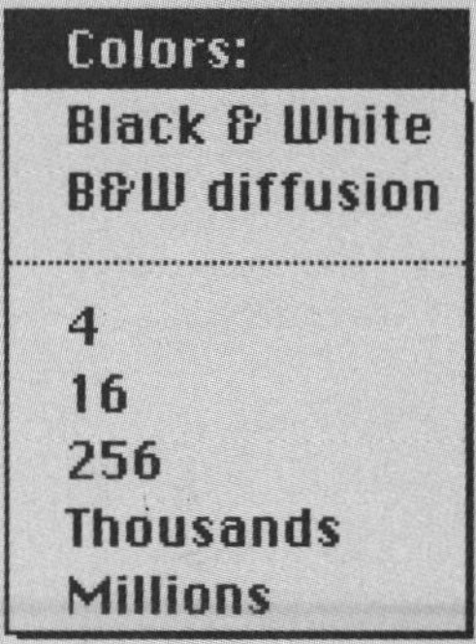

Another difficulty with working with graphics, especially in high resolution and with 24-bit true colour, is that the file sizes become huge. A 24-bit full colour scan of even a postcard sized image can take up megabytes of storage space, and will probably be too big to store on a single floppy disk. It's a good idea to invest in a removable cartridge type drive, so that when one cartridge is full you can simply stick another one in the slot and continue to save your work in an accessible form. Another solution is to invest in image compression hardware, which will probably be available from the people who supplied your screen. This can reduce the size of image files by around 20 times without reducing the quality of the image, and means that images will not only take up less space but be quicker to display.

Working with graphics on computers, especially complex colour graphics, can cause some difficulties but the advantages of flexibility and space to experiment are undoubted, although you won't think so when your computer has crashed just as you were about to save an afternoon's work. If you move to full desktop reproduction, where all the images in your document are processed and separated into their colour components by your computer, you will find yourself saving time and money. As this technology is as yet in its infancy, you also have the cheering prospect of both hardware and software becoming easier to use and more sophisticated and reliable.

THE SIMPLEST form of computer graphic is the bitmapped image, which comprises of a pattern of dots called pixels (picture elements) either created through a painting package or scanned into the computer. A wide range of computer tools, imitating the conventional ones, is available in paint packages to work on images. More sophisticated manipulation is available through specialist image retouching programs.

Select areas with rectangles (the marquee), freehand shapes (the lassoo) or by similar tint (the magic wand).

Fill areas (the bucket), sample colour or tint (thermometer)

Draw with freehand lines (the pencil), smoothed lines (the brush), straight lines (line tool), flowing paint (the airbrush).

Draw filled and unfilled rectangles (or squares), rectangles with rounded corners (roundrects) ellipses (or circles) and polygons, see right...

Rub out areas, blur, sharpen, and smudge (from one place to other). See right: first column; before, second column; after blur, sharpen, smudge.

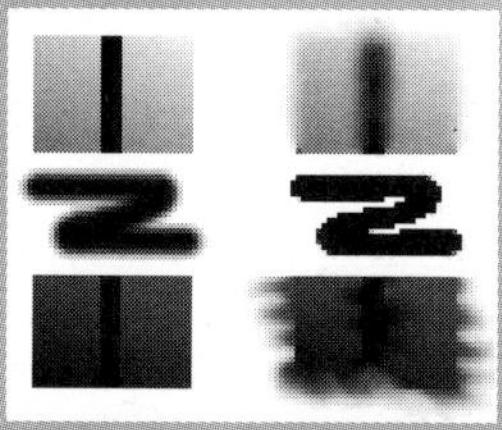

In practice you'll find yourself scanning in pictures and modifying them. Remember that the screen will not show all the detail in the picture, because it has a lower resolution and the dots the picture is made up of will be visible, an effect called pixellation.

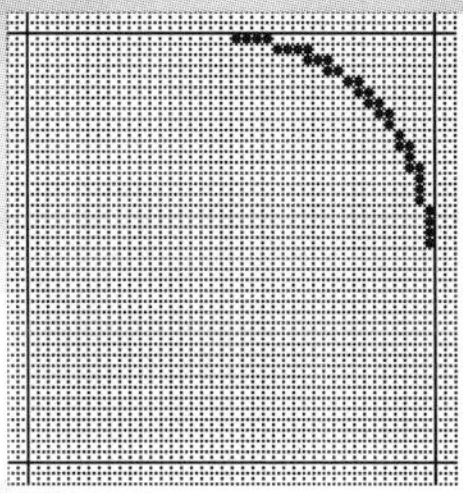

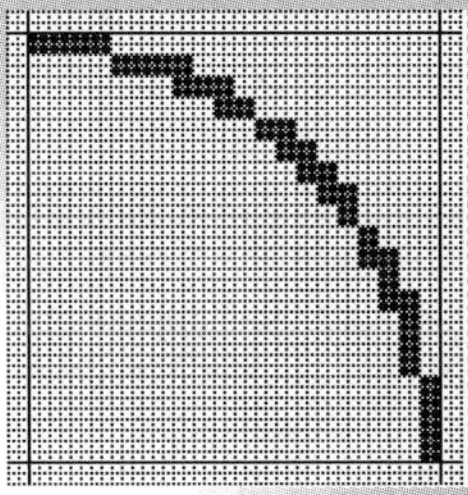

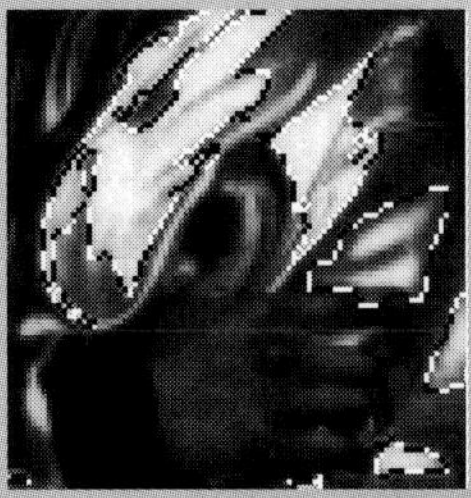

Bitmaps are grids of picture elements (pixels) which can be assigned colour values. Various tools can be used to create shapes out of the available pixels. Areas of colour can be resized and enlarged. A problem with bitmaps is that they do not bear enlarging, because the pixellation becomes more apparent.

Bitmap-oriented programs can select areas of the picture by enclosing them in shapes, either predefined or freehand, or by selecting colour values such as 'all the pixels near this one whose range is between these two values'.

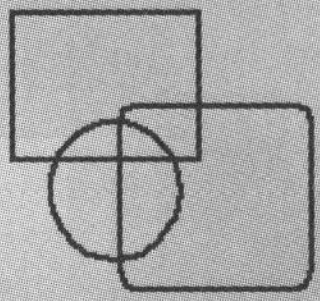

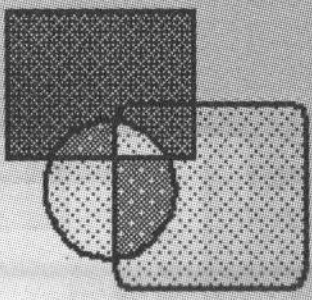

Shapes once drawn on the grid are areas of dots. Each area of solid tone can be filled in, or lines deleted and then areas filled in. When scaled down, the darker pixels crowd the lighter ones.

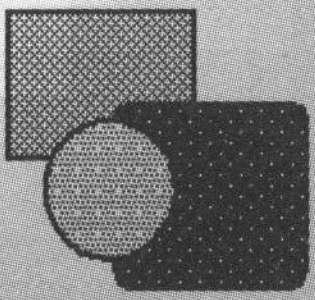

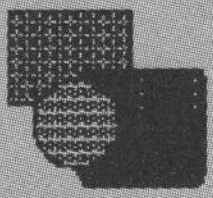

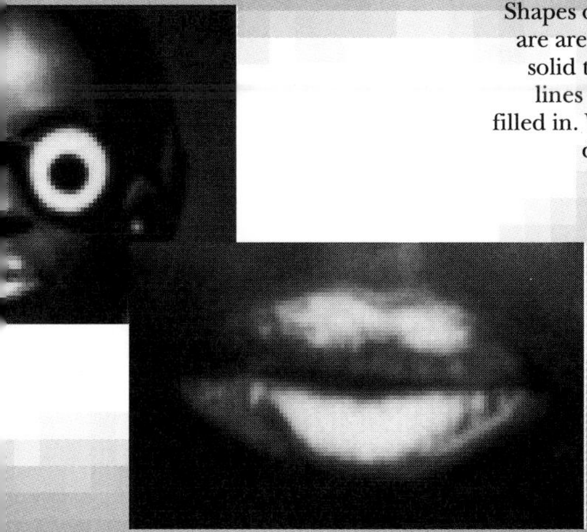

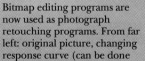

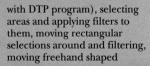

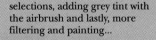

Bitmap editing programs are now used as photograph retouching programs. From far left: original picture, changing response curve (can be done with DTP program), selecting areas and applying filters to them, moving rectangular selections around and filtering, moving freehand shaped selections, adding grey tint with the airbrush and lastly, more filtering and painting...

OBJECT-ORIENTED drawing packages use a more sophisticated approach to representing images on the computer screen, remembering their shapes as objects and combinations of related elements rather than as a collection of dots. This gives the skilled operator much more freedom for creative expression; it also produces images which can be resized or distorted much more easily and effectively.

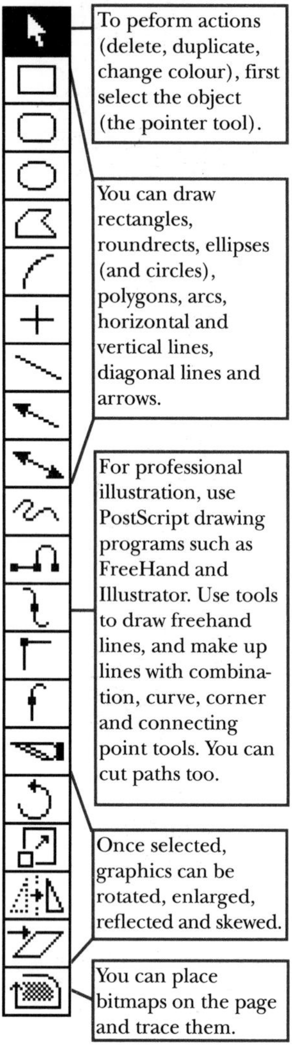

To peform actions (delete, duplicate, change colour), first select the object (the pointer tool).
You can draw rectangles, roundrects, ellipses (and circles), polygons, arcs, horizontal and vertical lines, diagonal lines and arrows.
For professional illustration, use PostScript drawing programs such as FreeHand and Illustrator. Use tools to draw freehand lines, and make up lines with combination, curve, corner and connecting point tools. You can cut paths too.
Once selected, graphics can be rotated, enlarged, reflected and skewed.
You can place bitmaps on the page and trace them.

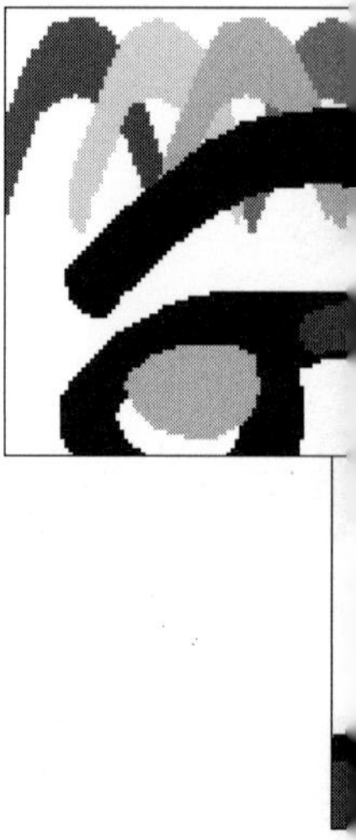

PostScript graphics programs allow you to make up shapes using lines that have straight and curved segments. You can edit curve points by dragging on handles attached to the tangent of the curve at the point. Connector points have a single handle which define the stress of the curve attached to the line (the position of the other point on the straight line effects the shape of the curve).

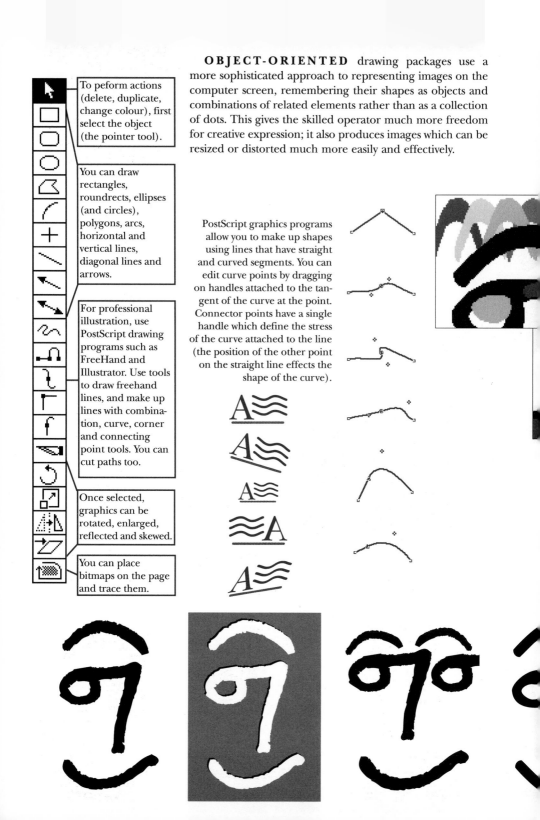

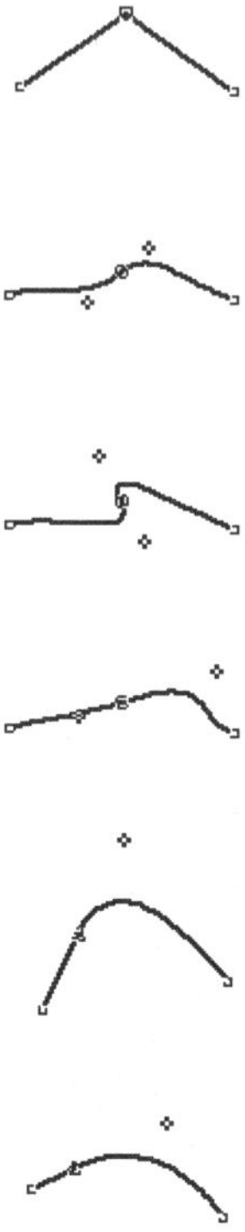

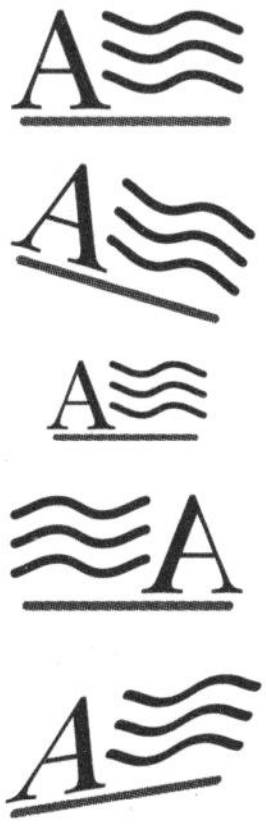

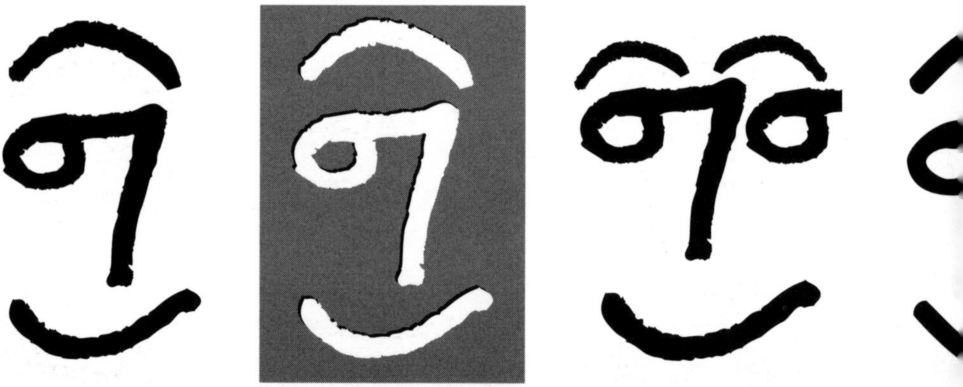

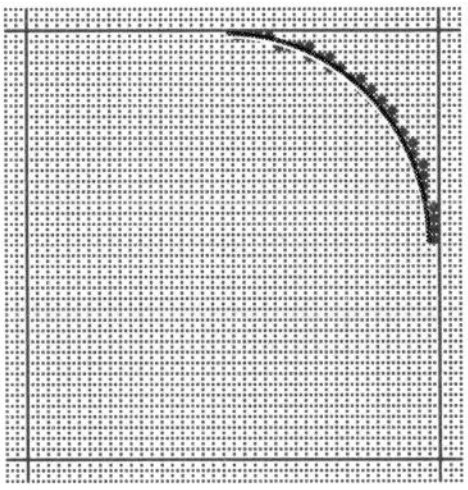

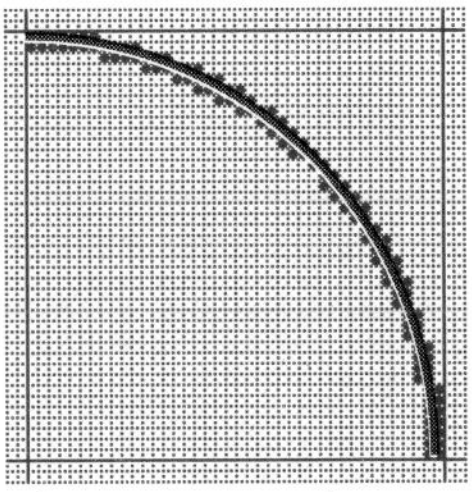

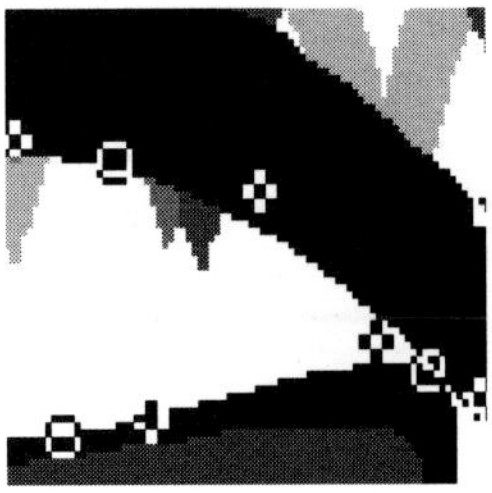

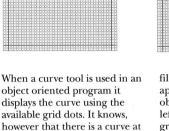

When a curve tool is used in an object oriented program it displays the curve using the available grid dots. It knows, however that there is a curve at that position, so when tools such as enlarge are used, it resizes the underlying curve, then works out which dots to fill in to display it. That also applies when looking at the objects at a larger scale (see left) – enlarge first then fill in grid. Parts are selected by logical element. Above right shows some outlines selected (round point markers show that it's made up of curve points).

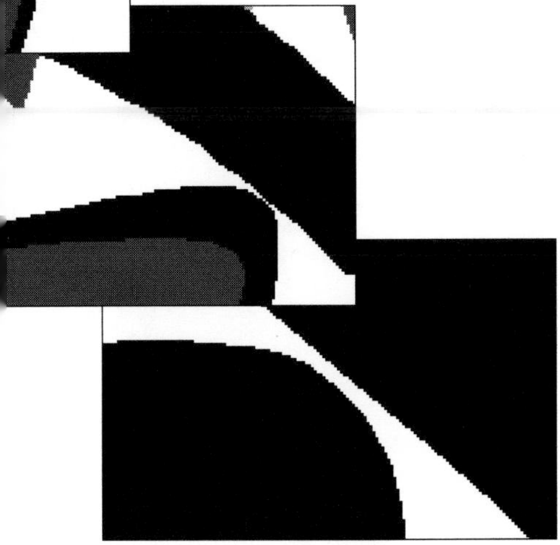

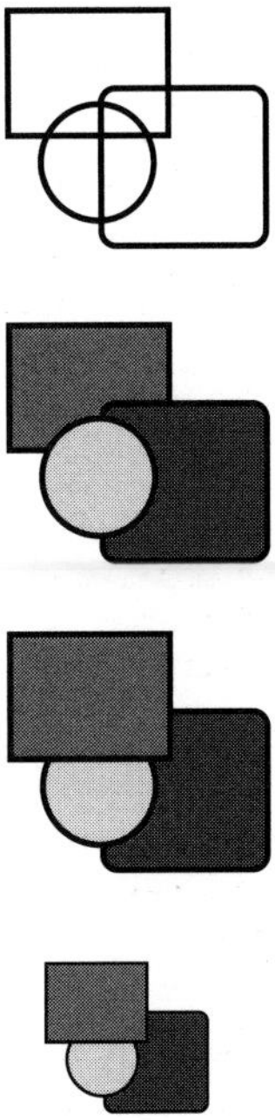

Object-oriented graphics programs divide a picture into its logical components (such as a circle on a rectangle on a rounded rectangle, which might be a company logo). These can be filled in, sent to the front or the back of the image, or combined into groups which always move together, making the scaling of images easy.

You can start your illustration by scanning artwork: 1. Original (from 10/01 proofreader's marks) (2) add a white copy and fill in background (3) add another copy (4) trace object and smooth. (5) Copy parts, change their colour and redistribute (6) Create a pattern out of one section. (7) Change borders, paste objects inside other objects...

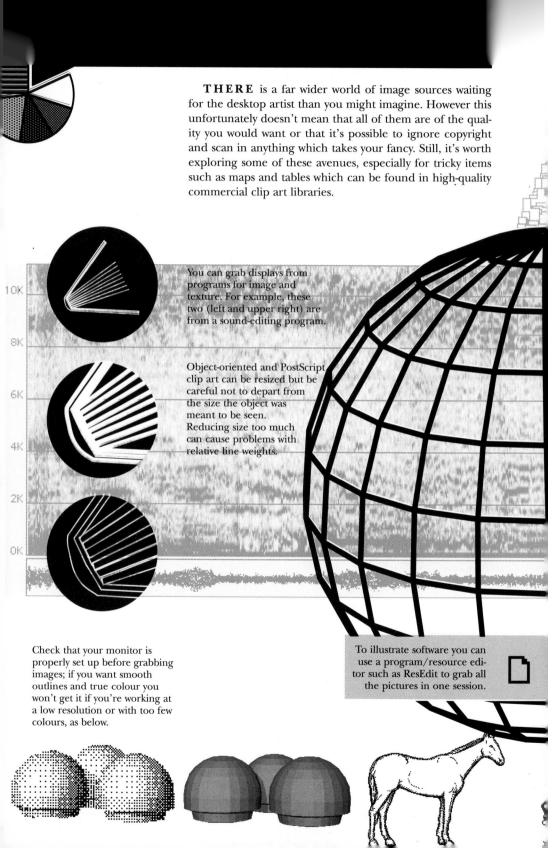

THERE is a far wider world of image sources waiting for the desktop artist than you might imagine. However this unfortunately doesn't mean that all of them are of the quality you would want or that it's possible to ignore copyright and scan in anything which takes your fancy. Still, it's worth exploring some of these avenues, especially for tricky items such as maps and tables which can be found in high-quality commercial clip art libraries.

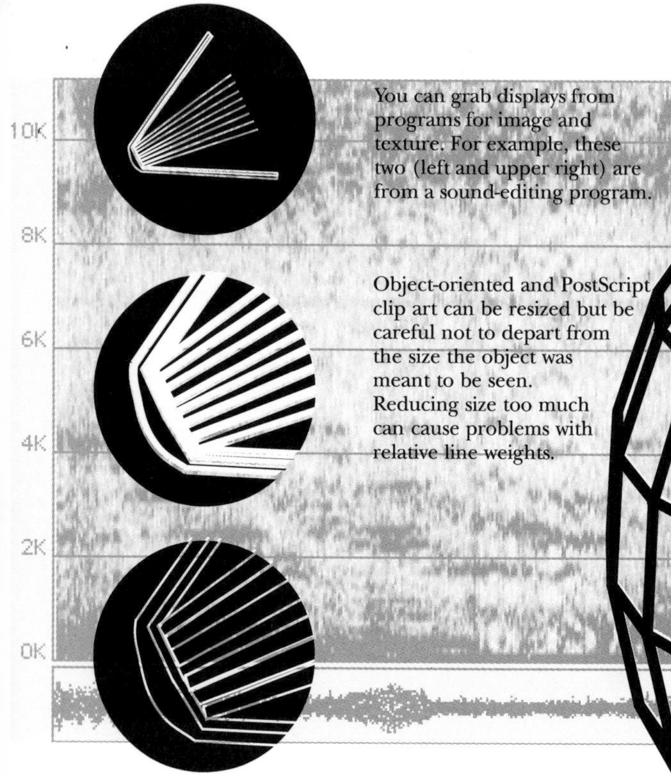

You can grab displays from programs for image and texture. For example, these two (left and upper right) are from a sound-editing program.

Object-oriented and PostScript clip art can be resized but be careful not to depart from the size the object was meant to be seen. Reducing size too much can cause problems with relative line weights.

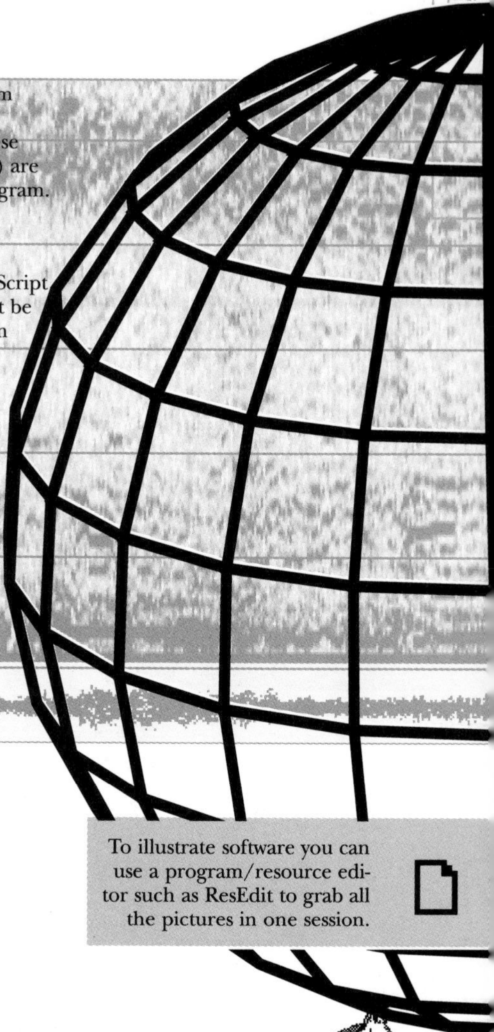

To illustrate software you can use a program/resource editor such as ResEdit to grab all the pictures in one session.

Check that your monitor is properly set up before grabbing images; if you want smooth outlines and true colour you won't get it if you're working at a low resolution or with too few colours, as below.

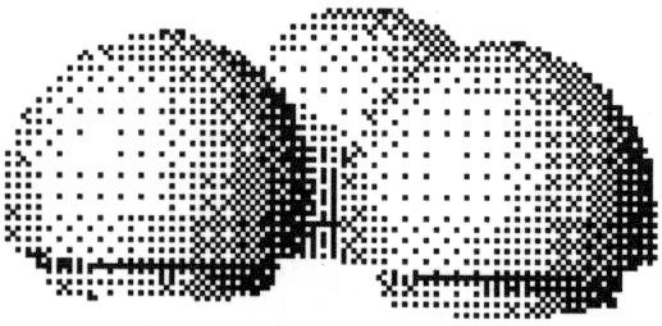

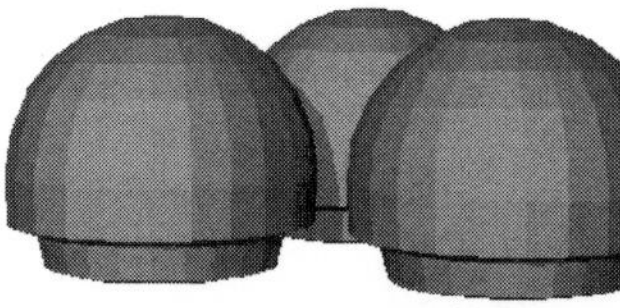

Value	J. Artichoke	Pink
Nick	40	34
Alex	26	47
Lynn	23	55
Paul	27	62
Dave	43	47
Amanda	60	30

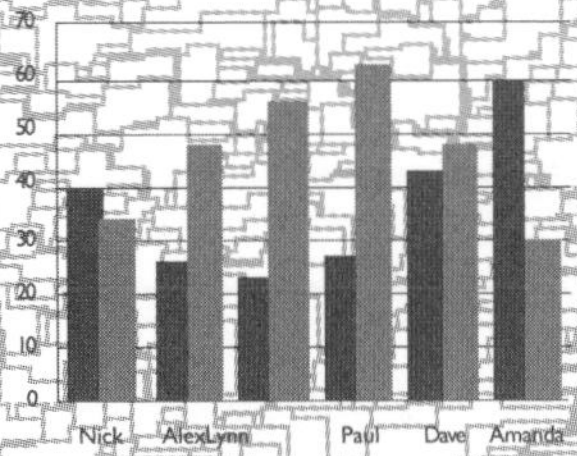

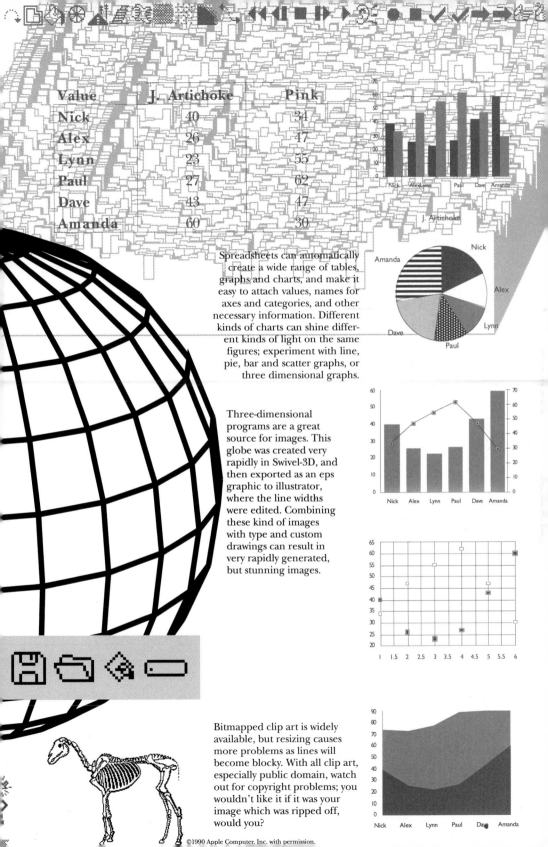

Spreadsheets can automatically create a wide range of tables, graphs and charts, and make it easy to attach values, names for axes and categories, and other necessary information. Different kinds of charts can shine different kinds of light on the same figures; experiment with line, pie, bar and scatter graphs, or three dimensional graphs.

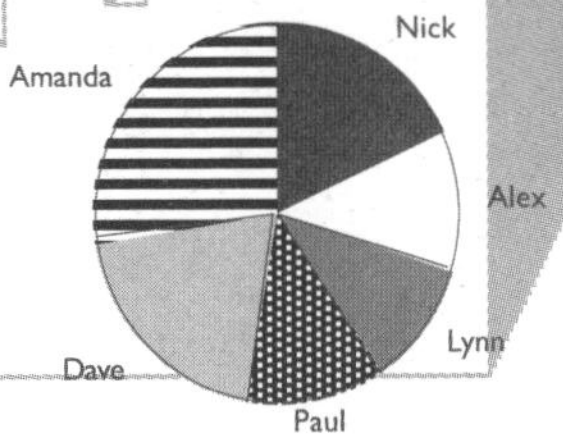

Three-dimensional programs are a great source for images. This globe was created very rapidly in Swivel-3D, and then exported as an eps graphic to illustrator, where the line widths were edited. Combining these kind of images with type and custom drawings can result in very rapidly generated, but stunning images.

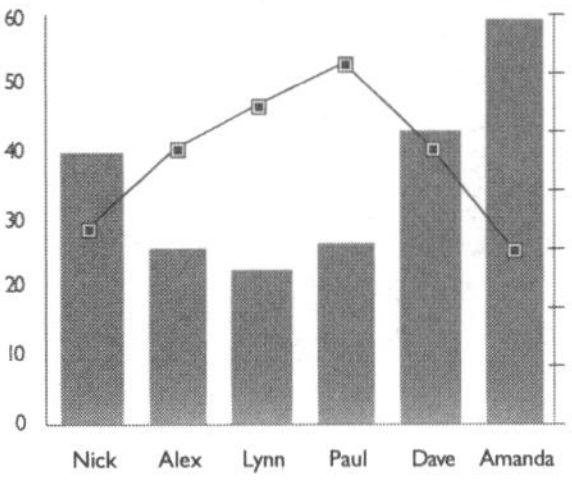

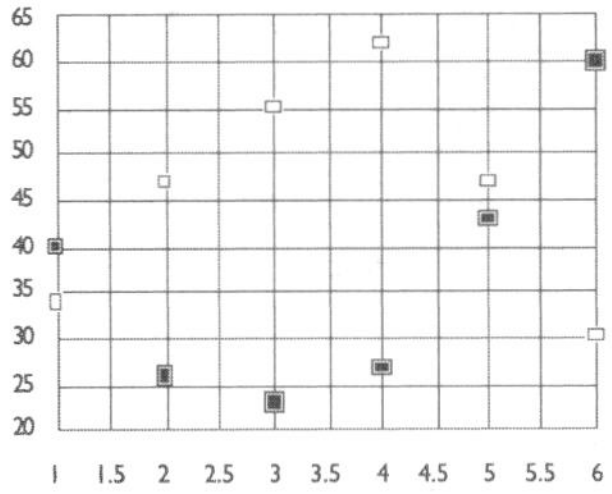

Bitmapped clip art is widely available, but resizing causes more problems as lines will become blocky. With all clip art, especially public domain, watch out for copyright problems; you wouldn't like it if it was your image which was ripped off, would you?

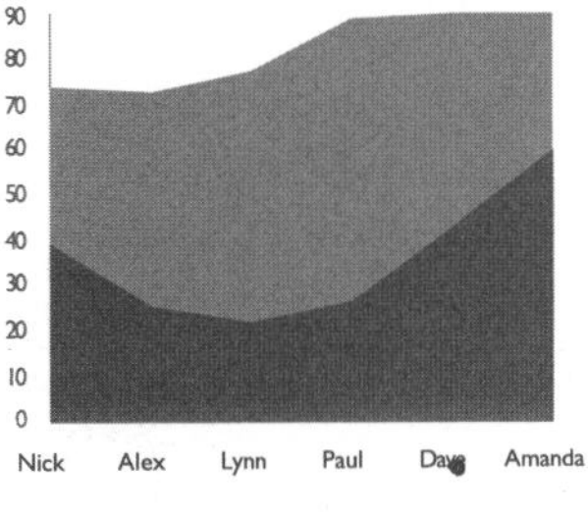

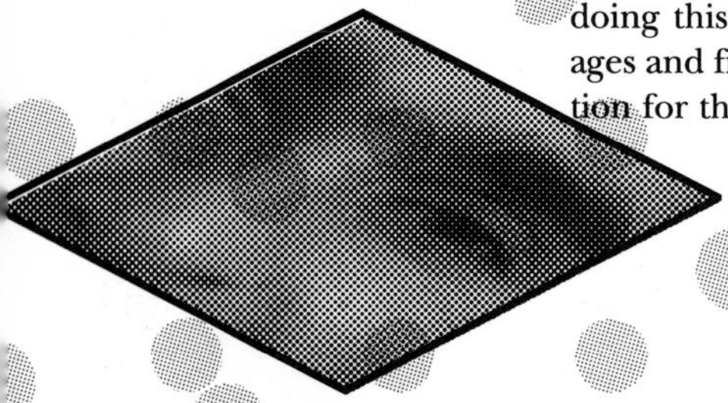

GETTING images in and out of computers is a more complex process than it might be. The computer understands only series of dots, or equations describing a line or curve, and this has to be translated from the image you want to see on the screen. Naturally there are several ways of doing this, which results in a wide choice of software packages and file formats, forms of encoding the image information for the computer's benefit.

16 Grey Levels

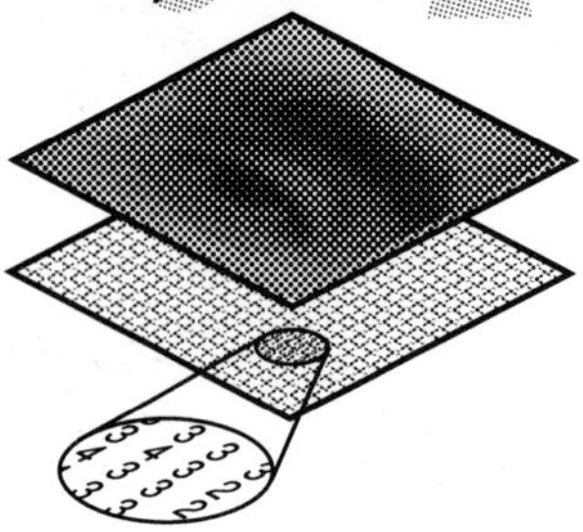

256 Grey Levels

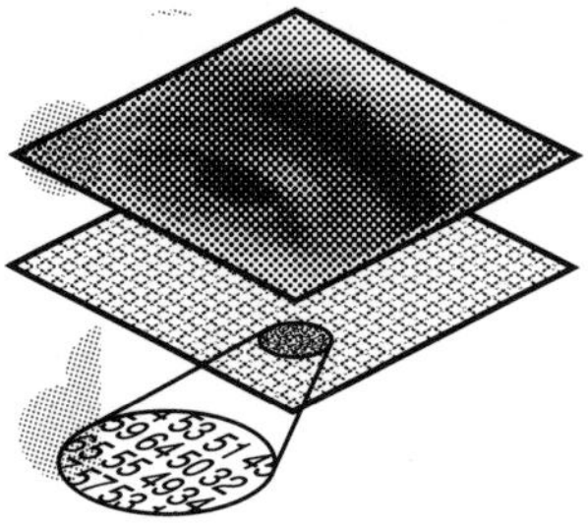

1 bit (black & white) dither

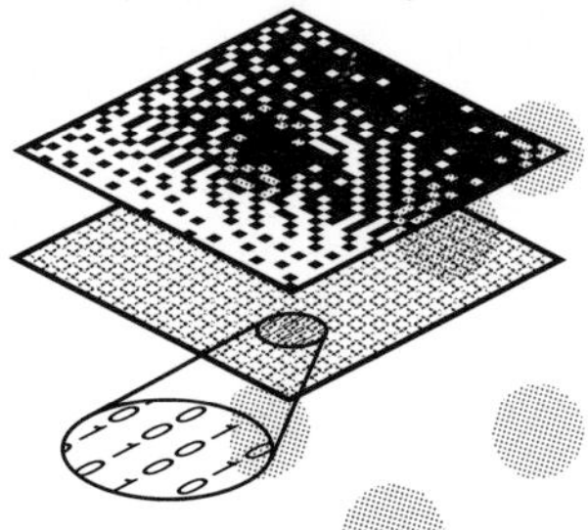

Computers store pictures as grids of numbers. You can choose the number of grey levels between black and white that the computer can display, depending on your hardware. The more grey levels the better the quality of the image, but the more space it takes to store. If you are using no grey levels the computer can dither the image with patterns of black and white to represent different levels of greyness.

To display different shades of grey using only a single ink, printers screen the picture, placing a grid of different sized dots to vary the intensity of the colour printed. Your computer can do this for you either on input or output. You have more control over this 'dithering' when you input the picture, but it makes it harder to resize it later – the size of the pixels that create the image become larger as you resize the picture.

Some scanning or graphics programs allow you to choose or even to edit a variety of dithering patterns and assign them to different grey value inputs.

Check out which file formats your applications can read and write, and tell everyone who needs to know which is best to use. Often you can use a third program to translate a file from one application to another – Adobe PhotoShop is an example of an application which can read and save many formats.

You can use graphic programs to dither grey-scale images. You can choose the resolution of the resulting 1-bit image as well as the form of dithering. Diffusion dithering gives a smooth texture using only black and white pixels.

(1) 50% threshold conversion – all grey values above 50% are changed to white, all below are set to black. (2) Diffusion dither at 75 dpi, (3) at 150 dpi and (4) at 300 dpi.

The main file formats, such as TIFF, RIFF and PICT are accessible from many programs, but none has emerged as a standard. Which one is best for you – which saves images in the least space, loads and saves them most quickly, or outputs fastest on the imagesetter – is best found out through trial and error, but it's worth standardising to minimise translation problems. Apple's PICT format can be read by most Mac programs, making it easy to swap images between applications. However, it uses instructions that are in the Mac's ROM chips to compress images. If you want to have your files worked with on other types of machines you would be better to use the less proprietary TIFF format.

New formats for compressing images are coming to market including JPEG. Some computers are equipped with hardware chips that can compress and decompress images according to this standard. This dedicated hardware is virtually instant, compressing an image in a second that would take an hour to squash down within software on an unequipped machine.

There are simple methods of transferring images from program to program on the Mac; you can copy to the Clipboard and then paste into files in another program.

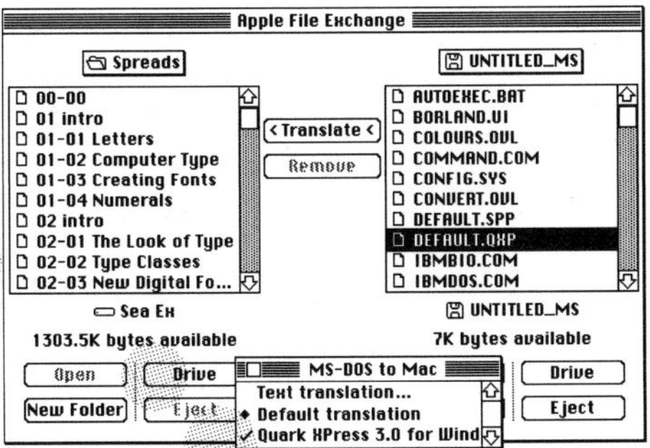

Text has as many problems as graphics when exchanging files between computers. But all is not lost in the file format world... there are translation programs to change the format of a file. For text, DataViz translators can sort out most problems; on the Mac, MacWrite II can read and translate a wide range of Mac and PC formats. If you end up with a disk which won't even fit in your drive, look in the back of a computer magazine and find a bureau which can read anything for you. With translated files it's doubly important to search for and replace linefeeds and any other peculiar codes which could have sneaked into the file.

7 Page layout

CREATING pages is the ultimate goal of most design involving type. Even if the end result will be something else, such as a three dimensional package or an image on a television or computer screen, type, images and the overall design will work together to produce the required effect or reaction from the reader or viewer. Working on the computer page layout is probably the first stage in creating the document where you will see the text set in the typefaces you have chosen.

Often a page design is intended to work not just in the current version but to serve as a template for future editions or following pages. Each fresh page then becomes a subtle variant of the original design, true to its intentions but never a slavish copy.

Desktop publishing makes it much easier both to create an entirely original design or to conform to design guidelines already established. An early criticism of DTP was that it allowed anyone to play with type and design and create anarchic documents using every typeface available on the computer in every size imaginable. It is easy to let the technology take control and use facilities just because they are there, but the skill with DTP is to use the computer to express your own design skills and intentions. While it's easy to use the computer to move columns of text and illustrations all around the page depicted on screen, in most cases you have to visualise the effect the design will have when it is reproduced on paper and discipline the design accordingly. However with DTP you see the results you will get immediately – a drop cap appears on the screen, a rule gains its real thickness, and so on, rather than having to wait for a proof to come back from the typesetters before you can see what your layout really looks like.

This flexibility is the cause of much of the trouble with DTP. When a headline busts – is too big for the space allocated – it's easier to set it a point size or two smaller so that it fits rather than go to the trouble of getting someone to rewrite it. It's quicker to justify columns of text vertically than to rethink the design or get extra text written. This is the kind of short cut which may very well be possible using DTP but which will not enhance the quality of your work. Leave these make do solutions to amateur newsletters and instead use the computer's power to create better design than you otherwise could have done.

One difficulty with laying out pages is that it's very easy to pick up and move objects on the page and to leave them in the wrong place. It's only too easy to forget to switch tools and to drag a column out of alignment when you meant to delete a couple of words. Use guidelines to ensure that the text in every column is correctly aligned, and that captions and illustrations are also properly aligned.

Small graphics which are mixed with text look good and modern but also tend to slip out of position. If it's possible with your DTP application, group objects together when you have positioned them so that you don't knock anything out of place. Other things to watch include kerning in large text sizes; DTP programs are notoriously bad at this, with one or two honourable exceptions, and you should look carefully at all headlines before letting them go.

the way you
Start off can a
readers will ap
text...

Signposts, symbols and other pieces of page furniture to help the reader find his or her way around the document are easily added using DTP, but make sure that they remain consistent throughout the document and that they aren't too overwhelming. The temptation to add too many finishing touches, such as the very much over used gradient fills behind boxed-out copy, should be avoided. Too many details and the page not only gets fussy but is more and more likely to go wrong at some later stage of the reproduction process.

The easiest way to ensure consistency in repeated designs is to use page templates and style sheets, which give you a page outline to start with and list all the design variants – rules, typefaces and sizes, symbols etc – that you are likely to need. Basing the design around a grid system also helps develop consistency, as headlines and illustrations will start at roughly the same level each time the design is used.

However templates are only of any use if the original design remains suitable for the material. Different types of document and different types of subject matter require a different approach; a solution which works for a poster won't necessarily work for a record sleeve, which has to make sense in different sizes. And a book will need another approach again. Make sure that you're making the best choices for the document in hand.

BASING page layouts on a grid system is a good way to bring order, coherence and consistency to related designs. As well as the vertical discipline imposed by the columns of text, horizontal grid lines help you to position illustrations and graphics correctly, and begin new chapters or articles in the same place each time. But the grid system should be there for your benefit and should provide a framework for your design not a strait-jacket.

The simplest type of grid layout is the single column per page. This has some advantages; the long lines of text mean that space is economically used, but readability may suffer if the lines are too long.

Single column layouts are best for smaller page sizes, and easily-readable typefaces. Continuous text which will keep the reader interested from line to line – for example in books – works well presented like this.

The illustration shows the various features of a grid including crop marks and type area, the distance pictures need to bleed off the edge of the page, and alternative configurations of columns which are included in most grids for flexibility.

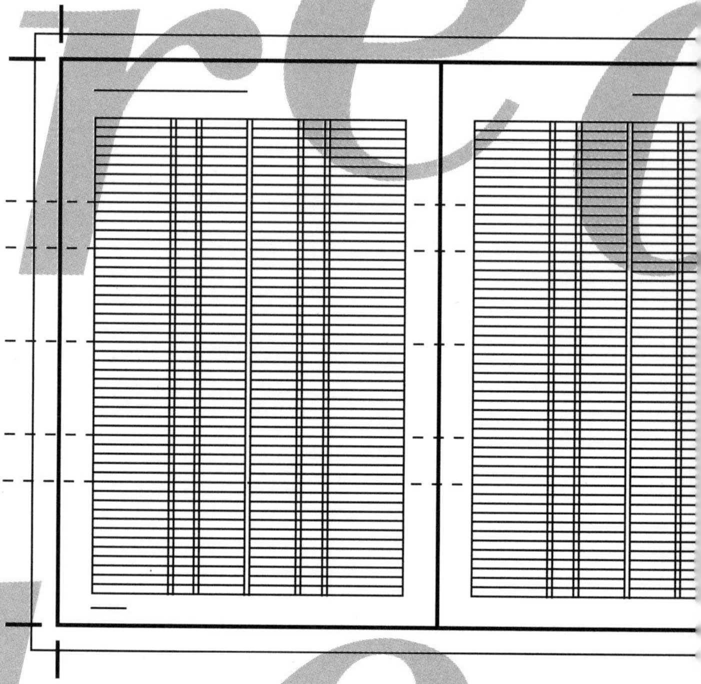

The horizontal part of a grid comes into play when more than one column is used. The horizontal grid divisions need to be fairly numerous – five rather than three, for example – or the page will look rather mechanical and it will be hard to fit illustrations naturally.

Two column grids work best where there is continuous text and a number of illustrations to bring in, for example in the feature section of a magazine. But the grid shouldn't visibly dominate the design.

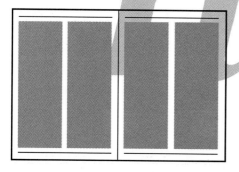

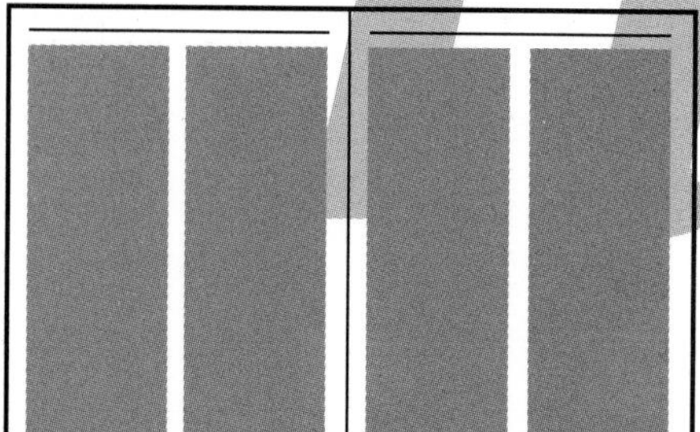

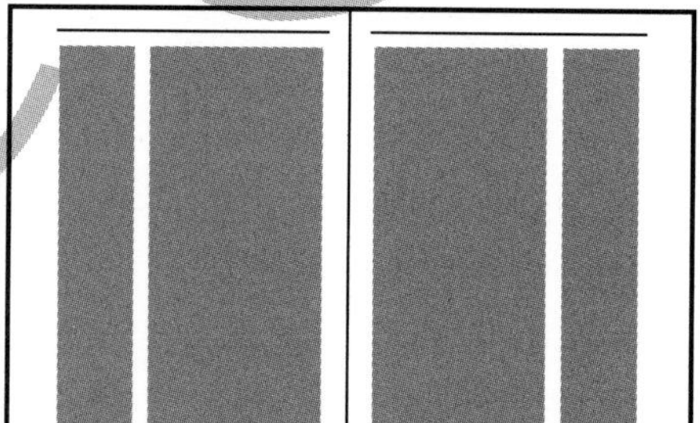

Newspapers and magazines, which need to keep to the same layout style every issue to create their identity and help their readers find their way around the text, are well served by the grid system of layout. Particularly in the large pages of a broadsheet newspaper, the discipline imposed by a grid helps make sense of the space on the page.

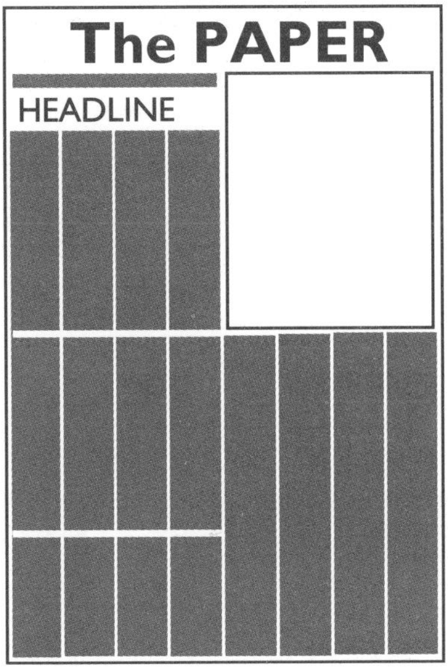

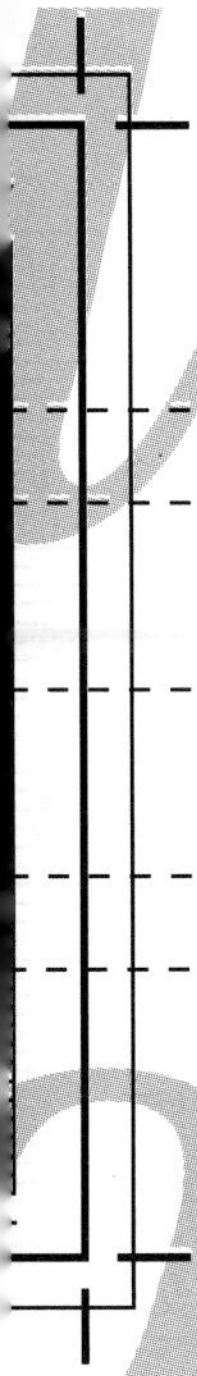

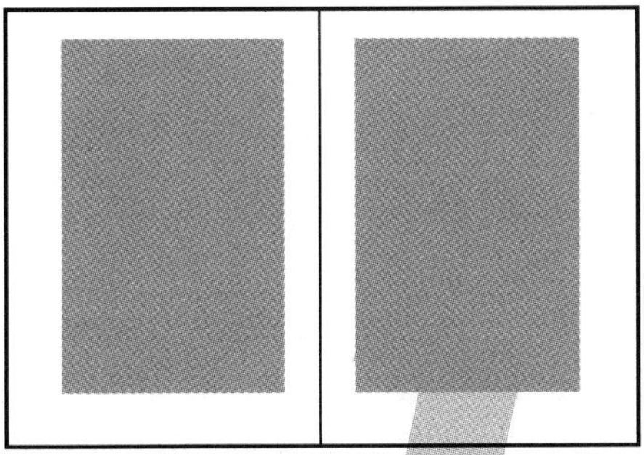

With a single column grid used for book design, features such as the balance of the margins, running heads and folios suddenly become much more important visually.

Three columns add liveliness and flexibility to a page. The narrower columns may need a smaller type size, or type ranged left for readability. The grid imposes discipline on what could be a confusing design; leaving white space helps the reader. This grid is ideal for text with lots of illustrations and box-outs.

Four columns is the greatest number generally practical in an A4 magazine. It’s best for busy opening news sections full of short text items and illustrations; dictionaries, directories and indexes also work well in this style where the short lines of text use space very economically.

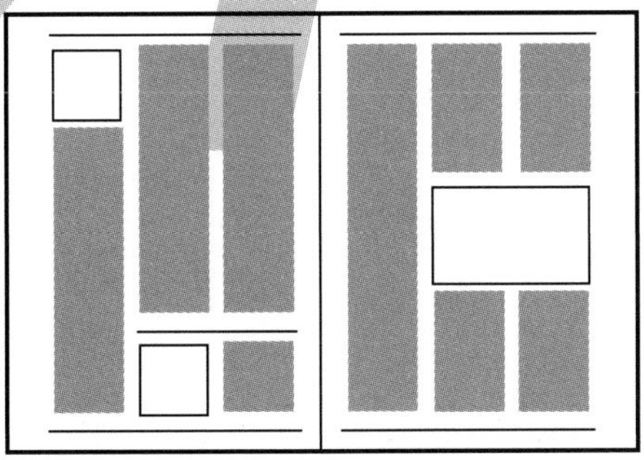

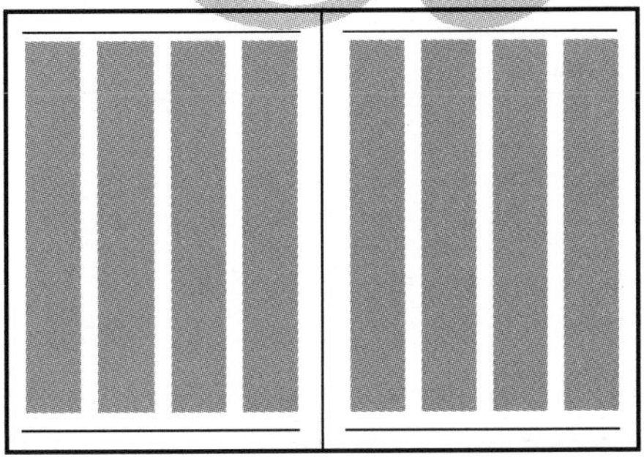

HEADLINES are the traditional way of indicating the beginning of an article and grabbing the readers' attention. To help make them as vigorous and dynamic as possible, typographers have designed special display faces, which are usually chunkier, blacker and bolder than text faces, to maximise impact. The size of the headline also shows how important a story is, and subheadings provide an at-a-glance index to a longer, more complicated story.

h e a d

PHEW!

A SCO

Balancing headings is difficult and requires skill on the part of the writer. Lines should ideally match up in length, and if they can't be matched, the top line should be longest, to create a reverse pyramid shape.

Consider variety in your headings and subheadings. For newsy layouts you'll need several sizes of heading – three on A4 pages, more on tabloid or broadsheet – to reflect the importance of various stories, and for other types of layout you'll also need different styles, to avoid monotony.

HOW MANY LEVELS

of headings

and subheadings

does a document need?

PHEW! WHAT A SCORCHER!

Headlines are supposed to grab the readers' attention, but the boldest, blackest type available may be overkill or else illegible. Balance the blackness of the heading to the rest of the page; a tightly kerned, ultrabold upper-case heading will swim aimlessly in a loosely designed page of white space. Remember that in some typefaces the differentiation of characters, such as 'O' and 'D', can be impaired by all that boldness.

i n g s

WHAT

RCHER!

CAPITALS or Upper and lower-case…Serif or sans serif…**bold or**

l e t t e r s p a c e d ...

Choosing between caps or upper and lower-case naturally depends on your document. Caps work best for short punchy headlines, but are harder to read for longer headings. Compare the headline style of tabloid and broadsheet newspapers.

Weigh up the suitability of a serif or sans serif typeface for your purposes. Sans is favoured for a cleaner, more modern look, but many of the better headline faces are tired and overused. Serif faces can convey a look of authority and importance.

Letter-spaced type is an excellent alternative to bold for introductory paragraphs, contents pages and tables of contents, provided it is given plenty of space. Experiment with mixing the two.

GET OFF to a good start by using big bold capitals. This traditional form of decoration tells the reader where to begin reading, gives a focus to the page and adds colour to the text. However, drop capitals aren't the only way to begin; a standfirst of larger text, small caps or a wider measure, or any combination of these, offer another way to set off in style. Symbols or other forms of decoration are another option.

The important thing is to make the opening of an article make a statement, and the blackness of a drop capital is the easiest way to do it. You could even pick out the letter in a colour which matches any illustration used. Modern bitmap faces make particularly good drop capitals.

It's easy to make raised caps using the latest versions of most DTP software. Starting the capital from the baseline of the first line of text works well, especially with vertically stressed letters such as this I.

VARIOUS letters of the alphabet are shaped so that the text really ought to flow around them rather than leaving a large white gap, as this example illustrates.

A POINT to consider is whether to leave a space after drop capitals which form a word in themselves, such as A and I.

I THINK it's usually better not to, but try it each way for effect.

the way you
Start off can
readers will a
text...

¶ Why not start off with a flourish?

For short items, of which several appear on a page, some kind of bullet point, either a simple blob or a typographic device such as the paragraph, is a good way to start without letting any single item dominate.

IT MAY be more effective to reverse out a drop capital, and easier to use, as the square box sorts out any problems with text flow.

Three and five lines are usual sizes for drop capitals, whether reversed out or not. It is usual to put the first few words in capitals, because it is easier to cross-align the top of the drop-cap with the uniform letter height of capital letters.

IF THE first paragraph starts like this, then…

The following paragraphs should either be indented, or…

There should be a line space between non-indented paragraphs.

ffect the way proach your

You should also consider whether to use a different typeface for the drop cap; a more decorative or contrasting font, such as a serif drop cap with a sans face, or a stylised bitmap face. News stories and chapters of books often begin with the first two or three words in caps, fairly heavily spaced, and with every line in the first paragraph full out.

The following paragraphs should be indented, or you should leave a line space between non-indented paragraphs.

GRAPHICS and symbols play a large role in shaping text and images into magazines, posters, record sleeves or whatever. They are the signposts which enable a reader to navigate from one end of an article to another – not a simple task in a glossy magazine where adverts can mean that one feature spans many pages.

Page straps form a clear beginning to a page and show that all the items on that page are part of a particular subject or feature, for example in a review section in a magazine. Combine graphics and text to the desired effect.

This is an example of a page strap

Continued on page 83

lived happily

Folios or page numbers are used in many kinds of documents and are vital for readers to find their way around. They needn't just be plain numerals, but need plenty of space so that they don't look as if they're about to fall off the page, and should remain consistent throughout the document. Convention is to place numbers at the top of the page in newspapers and at the bottom in magazines.

-1-

13

IIX

Icons, whether purely graphical or incorporating words, can identify different chapters of a book or sections of a magazine, or introduce warnings or additional information in a manual. They mimic the visual interface provided by computers like the Macintosh and the wordless symbols used by transport authorities.

Bullets to introduce or separate text items can be plain or decorative; they look best the same size as a small cap in the typeface being used.

Continuation and page turn symbols help readers to navigate through features. An arrow or pointer is much more effective than words. Try customising signposts to fit with your document, eg aeroplane page turn signs for an in-flight magazine. The same applies to end-icons which end an item or feature; creating and using one to fit your document adds to its identity.

Continued from page 82

ever after ■

Images can replace words, for example this telephone icon which could introduce a phone number or additional information.

** Footnotes must be accounted for when the initial grid is being created.

ILLUSTRATIONS are at least as important as words in creating the overall impact of a document, sometimes even more important. One of the best things about DTP is that it makes it much easier to combine text and graphics, to play about with their positions on the page and to do visually exciting things such as wrapping text around an illustration. In the old days, setting in bastard measures, as lines of non-standard length were called, was a difficult and time-consuming process. Now all you need to do is tell your computer how close the text should be allowed to get to the illustration, and click a couple of buttons.

For pictures which 'bleed' off the edge of the page allow a margin of about 3mm.

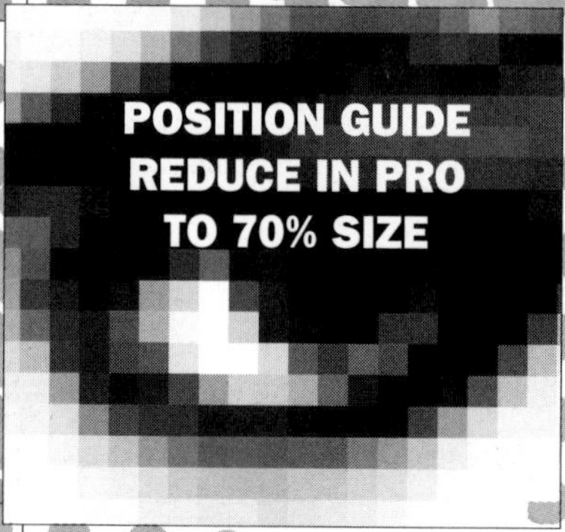

Scan in images at a low resolution to use as position guides for the printer, this way they don't use too much memory. Positioning and sizing of images is made much easier by this facility.

Different illustration formats such as PICT, TIFF and EPS files can all be used with page make-up programs such as Quark XPress and Pagemaker.

PICT information is stored in the document itself, and can inflate the size of your page layout documents.

Gratuitous Runaround

ILLUSTRATED here, one of the things that will really make your document look Desktop Published. A p o i n t l e s s runaround. with awful letterspacing! And widows. As any DTP salesman will tell you "It's so easy to place graphics on the page using DTP you can use more graphics more creatively. Illustrations can be placed in the middle of your text causing it to flow around the outline shape of the illustration. The picture box can be made 'runaround', so that the text flows around the shape of the box rather than the outline of the image. Picture boxes can be rectangular or circular."

Runarounds are great, and they have been used elsewhere in this book – when there was a good reason! Generally runarounds work best on circular objects.

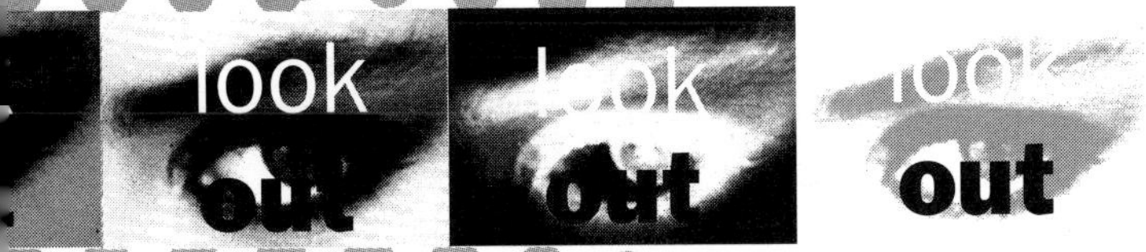
look
out
look
out
look
out

Even within the page layout package, certain types of image can still be manipulated. Altering the contrast curve, you can grey out or invert the image. It's also possible to stretch photos, as illustrated right, but you should have a reason for doing this rather than just because it's easy to do.

SPACE
CADETS
Apply now and beat
the rush for *your* place
on the shuttle

To have text boxed out of an illustration, the image is duplicated, and then the contrast curve altered for the copy of the image. The picture is then cropped as necessary to produce a box the right size to contain the image.

Frames for pictures can be selected and edited for style, colour and width, if you feel that any particular illustration needs a frame, or more likely, that an area of text needs to be bounded off from the rest of the page.

POSTERS are perhaps the best example of image and typography combined. The important thing is to make sure that these elements work together rather than separately to attract attention, the main function of most posters. The key-words are balance and impact. The size and style of text will probably be governed by the function of the poster; advertising hoardings which are driven past at speed need a simpler, more direct and less wordy approach than posters in tube stations where people have plenty of time to read the text and look at the image.

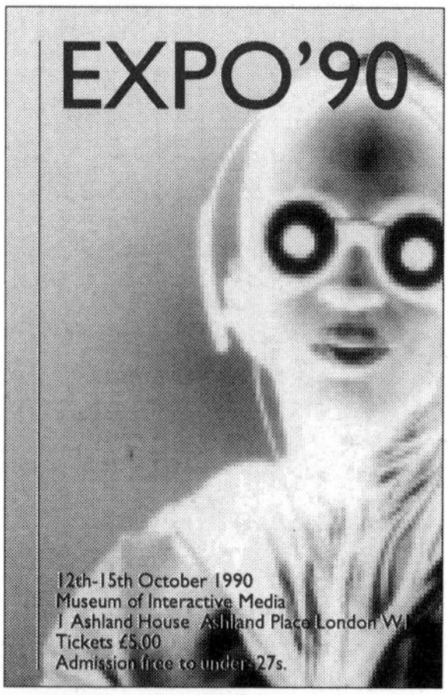
EXPO'90
12th-15th October 1990
Museum of Interactive Media
1 Ashland House Ashland Place London W1
Tickets £5.00
Admission free to under-27s.

EXPO'90
12th-15th October 1990 Museum of Interactive Media
1 Ashland House Ashland Place London W1
Tickets £5.00 Admission free to under-27s.

EXPO'90
12th-15th October 1990
Museum of
Interactive Media
1 Ashland House Ashland Place London W1
Tickets £5.00
Admission free to under-27s.

video text
computer
animation sound
How do you combine these into
MultiMedia?
Find out at MultiMedia 91
Conference and Exhibition
June 25-27 1991
Olympia 2 · London

The examples on the left show different approaches to poster design. Each gives different weight to the words and images. For an art exhibition you'd expect to see an example of the images on show on the poster, but a text-only version can work better in other situations.

Is the poster art or advertising? Perhaps it is both – if it's advertising a design company, for example. Other considerations are whether to use a photograph or a simple graphic, to let the image do the talking or add colour through a variety of text shapes and sizes.

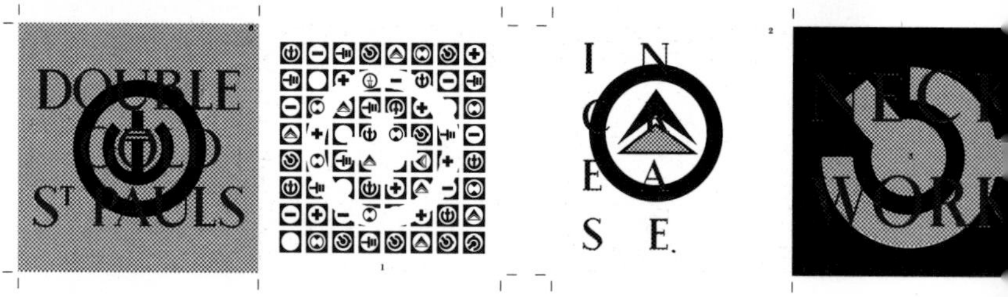

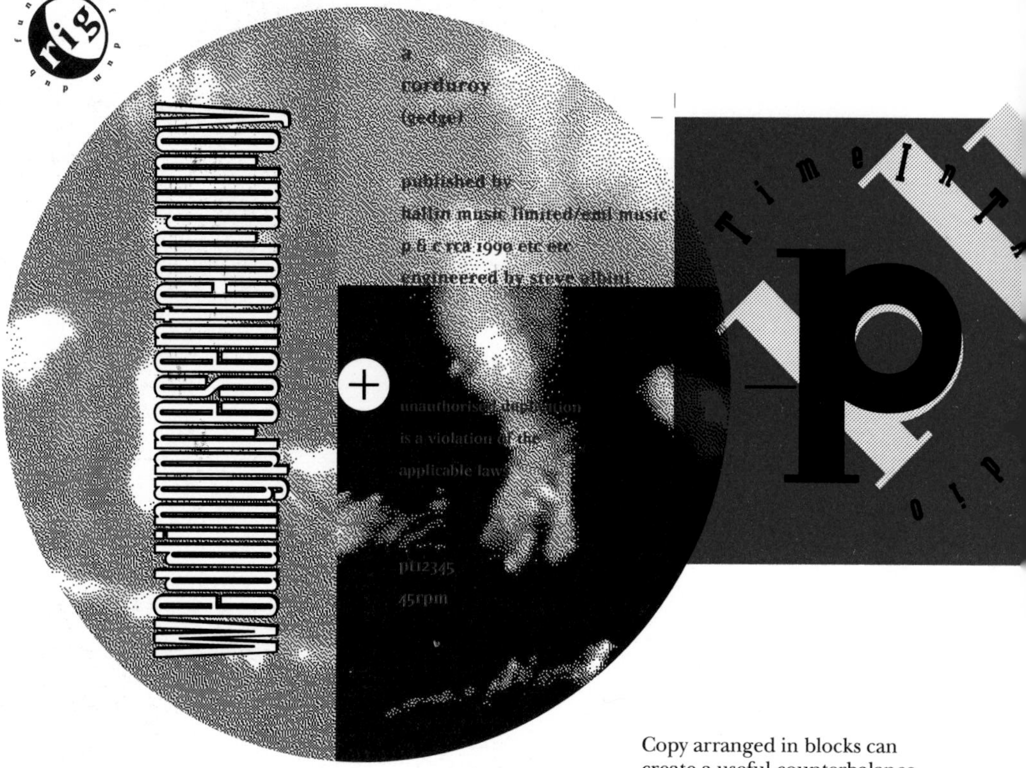

Designing record labels

It must be easy for disc jockeys to find the A-side, they are notorious for playing instrumental B-sides (and not noticing).

All sorts of copyright symbols, record company logos, details of song titles, authors and catalogue number must be found room on the label.

Designing record sleeves

Some of the information on a record sleeve is needed for legal reasons, eg notes about copyright, some of it is acknowledgements and thankyous. In general it is better to keep it discreet.

Copy arranged in blocks can create a useful counterbalance to pictures or more prominent text, such as the band's name or logo.

Text can also be arranged to evoke the mood of other forms of packaging.

The most important thing is that the sleeve should reflect the content of the record and be attractive to its potential market. Type style alone can distinguish dance music from jazz, from heavy metal. There are times when this is all that is available, or desirable.

designing a record sleeve

let's say

reward the persistent viewer

of record sleeves make sure

there is something new to see

second and third time round

little flourishes can greatly

However a good logo is important for bands; it creates an identity which can be used across a wide range of merchandising such as stickers and t-shirts, and it gives fans something to copy and emblazon on walls or across the back of their jackets.

There are no absolute rules.

Record companies like the band's name to appear across the top of the sleeve in big letters so that it's easy for fans to find the disc in record shops. However some bands prefer to be enigmatic and include as little information as possible on their sleeves.

8 Printing

ALTHOUGH printing is the final stage in the production process, it should be given careful consideration right from the outset of the design project. Your design must work within the constraints dictated by the print budget.

A document printed in one colour only is naturally less costly than a lavish full colour production. The paper you choose, reproduction of images and how you treat them, and any special effects you use all affect the overall cost. Remember, you don't need to spend a fortune on expensive printing effects to obtain a great result, so think hard about whether you really need them before you commit yourself.

It is important to make an appropriate choice of printer, so obtain quotations from more than one. Recommendations can be useful but look at examples of the printer's work. Quality and price vary widely. Different printers can submit significantly varying prices even when quoting on the same specification. There are several factors involved here, for example, it would not be cost effective to give a small one colour document to a printer who uses printing presses with the capacity to run five or six colour jobs. You will be paying for the additional costs of running a machine with excess capacity to your requirements. Alternatively your work may be 'farmed out' to another printer, again resulting in higher costs and loss of control over the printing of your design.

Printers in major cities are generally more expensive than out of town printers. Use an out of town printer if you have room in your schedule to allow for the extra delivery time.

Print specification

Title
Collier's Rules

Quantity
10,000

Size
234 x 156mm

Decide whether to supply the printer with bromides (camera ready artwork) or film, both of which can be run out from an imagesetter. If you send film to the printer it cuts out the bromide stage, but in spite of this advantage it is not always practical to do so. Discuss this with your printer. If you are supplying film instruct the imagesetting bureau as to whether you require film positive or negative, right reading or wrong reading; emulsion side up or down. Your printer will tell you what he requires, eg positive film, right reading, emulsion side down.

When making film, whether your imagesetter produces it, or whether you printer makes it by shooting the artwork with a special camera, continuous tone 'copy' (eg photographs) must be converted to *half tone*. As printing presses can only print solid colour the effect of tonal change is created by breaking the image into a series of dots of varying size. This is traditionally done by photographing the image through a screen. Screens have varying numbers of lines per inch; the more lines per inch, the finer the screen, the finer the reproduction quality. The screen you choose depends on the paper you are printing on and the printing conditions. A newspaper uses a coarse screen (maybe 80 l.p.i.), while a magazine uses a finer screen (up to 150 l.p.i.). Most Mac designers prefer to leave keylines as position guides for images, but all the photos in this book were scanned in, and set directly onto film. If you are supplying film with halftones to the printer, even if it is only tinted text like a heading in 60% black, remember to specify the screen to the imagesetting bureau.

Plates are made from film by raising, lowering or chemically treating the print area to differentiate it from the non printing area. There are four main printing techniques.

Letterpress is the oldest of the four methods. The raised surface of the area to be printed is inked, and the image is transferred from the printing plate onto the paper by pressure. The major disadvantage of this method is the length of time it takes to make the photoengraved plates.

Gravure also uses photoengraved plates, but the image is etched into the plate rather than raised out of it. The plate is inked and wiped clean so that ink remains only in the etched areas. When printed under pressure the paper draws the ink out of the lowered areas. This process requires that all copy, line and continuous tone alike must be screened.

Offset lithography (known as offset) is the most recently developed technique of the four. The metal plates are made photographically by a simpler process than the previous two methods. It is currently the most commonly used process, being relatively low cost and offers the designer creative freedom – a wide variety of finishes and subtle half tone effects being possible.

Silkscreen printing plates are less expensive than litho, but each print is more expensive, so this process is most suitable for small runs. Silkscreening gives very even solids, making it suitable for jobs such as large posters and printing onto fabrics like t-shirts.

Stock

text: 115gsm cartridge

colour sectio

115gsm gloss

cover: 240gsr

invercote boa

THE ORIGINAL design is governed by the printing budget. A design which consists of black and white line artwork is the cheapest to print. You must expect to pay more if you add one or two colours to your design, and more still if it is printed in full colour. Photographs and any other halftone images will also increase your printing costs.

Specifying your exact requirements to the printer and obtaining a quote should be done at the beginning of your design project. Go to more than one printer prices can vary widely, depending, for example, on the location of the printer. Choose a printer who offers a satisfactory compromise between quality and price.

Specify the quantity of documents you require. In general the price per copy decreases as the total quantity printed increases. If you are not sure, ask the printer to quote on several different quantities.

Give the printer precise measurements of your document. How long is your document? Will it be printed on one side only or both? Does it have a cover? Is the cover printed on the inside as well as the outside?

There is a bewildering array of papers and boards to choose from. Decisions must be made on colour, texture and weight. It is important to choose stock which is suitable for your document – extra impact can be added to your design by an appropriate choice. Ask paper merchants to send you paper samples of their ranges. Environmentally-friendly, recycled stock is widely available now and worth considering.

Print specification

Title

Collier's Rules

Quantity

10,000

Size

234 x 156mm (royal octavo)

Extent

144pp plus cover

Stock

text: 115gsm coated cartridge
colour section: 115gsm gloss art
cover: 240gsm invercote board

Printing

text: two colour throughout except one 16pp full colour plate section
cover: 4 colour, one side only

Finishing

folded in 32 page sections, sewn and covers drawn on at spine

Tell the printer how many colours you intend to print. Gold and silver are the most expensive colours to print.

If you intend to reproduce your document partially in colour, reduce your costs by planning your document so that images and text to be printed in colour fall together in sections, and inform the printer of this when you ask for your quotation.

Specify the method of finishing you require – what binding method do you want to use? Any special effects such as lamination or varnish must be included in your print specification. The printer also needs to know at this stage how the document is to be folded, or if perforations for a tear-off form are required. Show the printer a mock-up of the design.

If your job is a complex one it is advisable to include the cost of printer's proofs in your budget. This is your last chance to correct any errors, and to make sure that you are satisfied with the standard of printing.

Another factor which can add to your overall printing cost is an unusually-shaped document which requires special cutting, eg rounded corners or a pocket to be cut and folded and glued on a folder. Give the printer precise measurements. It is a good idea to provide a mock-up of the proposed design.

MARKING UP artwork accurately is vital to ensure that the printed job lives up to your expectations. It is your instruction to the printer, so make sure that it is clearly written and unambiguous. Size, colouring of typography, backgrounds, pictures and tints, picture sizes, bleeds, cutting edges, folds etc, must be specified on a tracing-paper overlay.

Before starting your mark-up, check the bromide carefully against your laser proof for any errors which may have crept in at the high resolution output stage. It is cheaper to correct errors now than after the job has gone to print.

When printing in colour it is essential that you give the printer precise colour references. Choose colours from a Pantone reference book – each colour swatch has a code which you must indicate on your overlay. Pantone books are divided into two sections showing colours on both coated and uncoated paper.

If the document is being printed in full colour all colours will be created from a combination of yellow, magenta, cyan and black – four colour process. Use a colour reference book to find out how the specific colour you require is made up from the four colours. Occasionally it may be necessary to specify a fifth 'special' colour which cannot be achieved through process colour. Make sure that you indicate its Pantone number.

You may not want to print all colours as 'solids'. You can indicate the strength of colour you want to achieve by specifying a percentage 'tint' of a colour, eg: 50% black will produce a mid grey, 10% red will produce a pale pink. Printing presses can only print solid colour, so a tint is composed of a series of dots, with a greater or lesser intensity of dots-per-inch, depending on the strength of tint required.

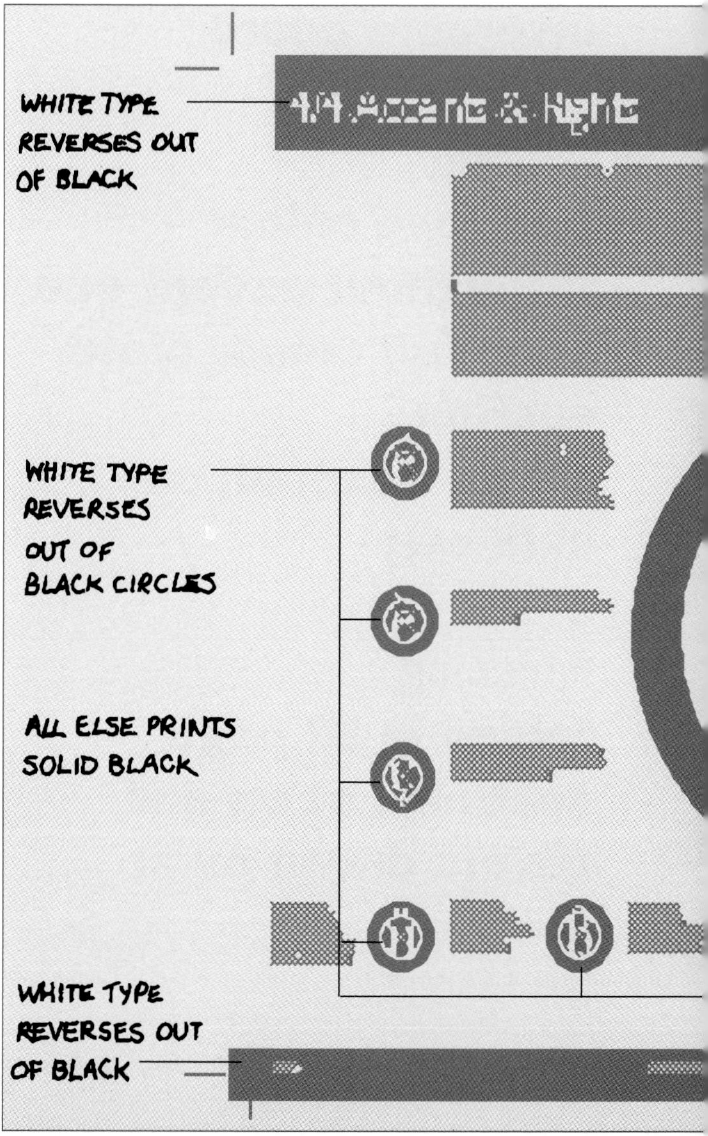

A variety of techniques can be used to reproduce photographs and illustrations.

Paste a position guide – a photocopy or tracing of the image to size – onto the overlay. Indicate how you want to crop the picture, if only a specific area of the original image is to be reproduced.

Precise measurements must be given (as a percentage or in millimetres) of the size you wish an image to reproduce at. If no enlargement or reduction is necessary, specify 'same size' (or 's/s.').

If it is to be 'squared up' (contained within a rectangular box), indicate whether or not you want your keylines to print.

You may not want the background of your original image to be reproduced. Indicate to the printer on your overlay the area of the image you want to print. This is called a cutout.

A vignette effect can be created by the printer. For example, the edges of a photograph can be faded out gradually.

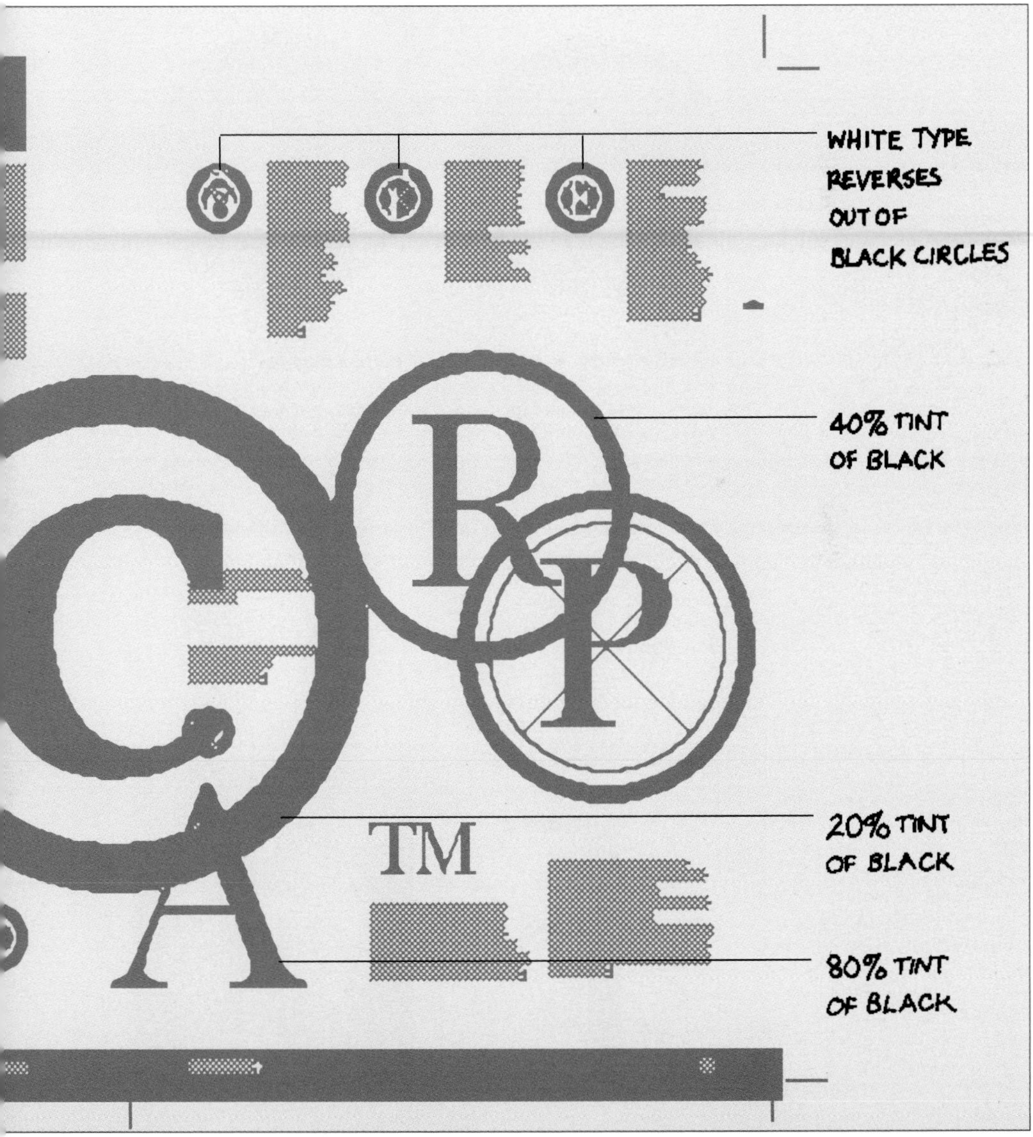

FINISHING processes should be selected on the basis of their suitability to a particular document. This depends on the use of the document (ie. whether it is an internal document or one for external publication); the size and thickness of the document, and practical usage – for example, is it important that the pages lie completely flat when open?

Printers can produce a huge variety of special effects, which, if used with care, can add individuality and quality to your design. They are invariably very expensive, however, so think hard about whether you really do want them before you commit yourself.

Envelopes
A variety of stock shapes and sizes are manufactured. They are cheaper and more quickly available than made-to-order envelopes. If a document is to be mailed out, it is sensible to design it to fit a standard size.

Saddle-stitching
Also known as wire stitching, this is one of the cheaper and more popular binding processes, suitable for pamphlets and catalogues.

Thicker documents which cannot be saddle-stitched could be side-stitched, although this method of binding has largely been replaced by perfect binding now.

Perfect binding
Increasingly widely used now, it holds the pages together and fixes them to the cover by means of adhesive. It is relatively inexpensive, used for documents such as manuals and paperback books.

Film
If film is to be supplied to the printer in place of bromides, make sure that you are instructed on the following technical specifications: orientation (right or wrong reading), position (emulsion-up or down), image (negative or positive). Specify these requirements to the imagesetting bureau who are producing your film.

right reading (readable)

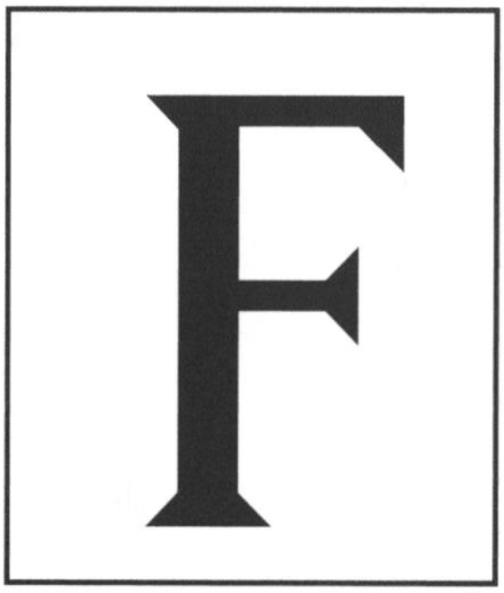

film negative

‘A’ size papers fold in half along their long edge to give the next smaller size. So fold A4 paper to get two sheets of A5.

International paper sizes

sheet size	millimetres	sheet size	millimetres
A0	841 x 1189	B0	1000 x 1414
A1	594 x 841	B1	707 x 1000
A2	420 x 594	B2	500 x 707
A3	297 x 420	B3	353 x 500
A4	210 x 297	B4	250 x 353
A5	148 x 210	B5	176 x 250

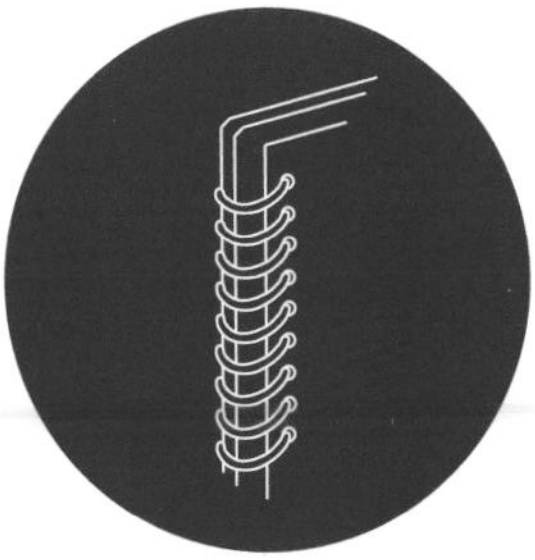

Spiral binding
Generally used for internal documents, although it has the considerable advantage for cookbooks and manuals of allowing the pages to lie perfectly flat.

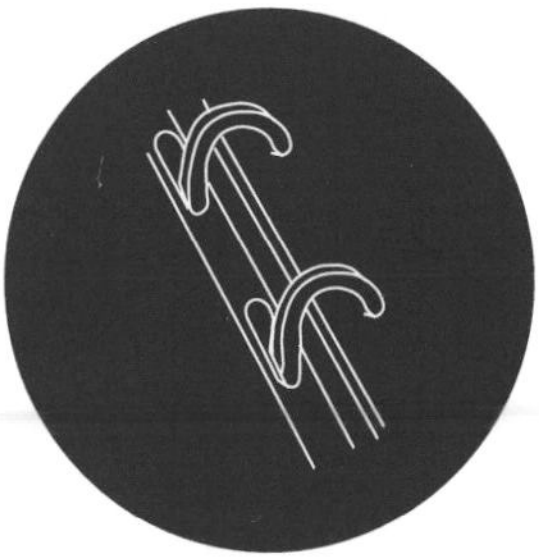

Ring binding
Suitable for looseleaf folders. Pages can be added whenever they are needed.

wrong reading (unreadable)

film positive

Special processes

Thermography
Creates a raised glossy image – be careful how you use it, it can look tacky.

Foil blocking
The printed image is a thin lamina of metallic foil, available in a wide variety of colours, particularly useful for creating a rich gold effect, for example.

Water marks
A subtle and understated way of giving a document distinction.

Die-cutting
Shapes cut out of card to form peep-holes. This lends a 3-D effect to the design. Remember to present an accurately drawn-up shape for the cutter template if you are going to use this technique .

Holograms (3-D photos)
Can be used in print processes but they are prohibitively expensive in the majority of cases.

Spot varnishing
This technique highlights specified features of a design.

Embossing
Raises the design from the surface of the paper, giving a tactile quality.

9 Colour

ANYONE WHO HAS produced black and white images using desktop computers will know that it is far from easy to get good results. Reproducing colour is even more difficult. Black and white images are regarded as simply giving an impression – a reader seeing colour will expect it to look like the real thing.

While it is exciting to see a full colour image on screen, getting it into print poses a number of difficulties. A computer monitor is a luminous medium mixing red, green and blue beams to create white. Conventional printing relies on light reflecting off inks, ideally with cyan, magenta and yellow combining to absorb all the visible light and thus appear black. Converting an image from one medium to the other is a haphazard process, partly due to a lack of standards in RGB monitor display. Another common problem is the patterns caused by the interplay of overlayed colour tints in the printing process. These patterns are known as moirés (pronounced mwar-ray); although common, significant steps have been taken to reduce them.

While programs may be able to automate some processes in colour reproduction, there is no substitute for experimentation and experience. Where possible controlled tests should be done to give some indication of what you can expect.

One reason for the popularity of desktop colour is the number of powerful graphics programs available, for instance Illustrator on the Macintosh and Freelance on the PC. These images are most easily dealt with separated straight from the computer that generated them. Unfortunately there are many colours a monitor can display that cannot be matched on press (the reverse is also true). Moirés are less likely if tints of no more than two of the process colours are used (three colours if one of them is solid).

For illustrators who want to use computers for artwork but don't want to get involved in colour separation, a good alternative is output to slide for conventional scanning. Comparatively this process gives very reliable results.

Input: Dealing with images that must be scanned introduces another dimension. They can be captured using transparency or flatbed scanners, grabbed using a video camera, or scanned on a high end system. This last option gives the possibility of taking a low resolution image from a colour house to be used for position and visualisation only, and sending back made up pages that, when output, link up with the high resolution original. This takes most of the difficulty out of the colour reproduction process and is an easy way in for most users. When looking at an input device, it is important to determine its resolution, the range of colour it can recognise, and its ability to capture detail, especially in areas of shadow. Images should be sampled at a greater frequency than the screen that will be applied to them, and this can result in very large file sizes, causing storage and processing problems. Image compression can help alleviate this, but be prepared to fork out for extra memory and hard disk space.

Prepress: Before a scanned image is output in page there are three processes most users will go through. Firstly, correcting errors produced in inputting (the 'fudge' factors); secondly, altering the image, either retouching or altering the colours; and lastly adjustments dependent on the way the image will be printed. For instance, compensating for the increase of dot size on press. This implies that the monitor and possibly the scanner have been calibrated.

Output: Producing usable film separations on an imagesetter requires close collaboration with your bureau and your printer. The bureau must know how to avoid the moirés often produced by PostScript interpreters, and maintain their imagesetter and processor carefully calibrated. Colour files can take ages to imageset (not least because there are multiple films per page) and a method for transferring large files must be organised. You should consult your printer about press characteristics before separating images, and about the film clarity and dot density required for plate-making from your output. Alternatively, show them some output to check these characteristics.

State of the what: the investment of time and money required for desktop colour makes it an option for the adventurous only. This leaves the option of producing some colour separations with the computer (areas of flat colour, computer generated artwork) and combining this with conventionally separated film from a colour house. There are a number of developers proposing device independent colour models (the equivalent to PostScript in the graphics market), interpreters for colour printers (similar to the Raster Image Processor), routines for device calibration and image compression, and links to high end output systems. These systems should make colour accessible to most users.

When there are more compact-disc based information systems, it will no longer be necessary to convert from the screen image you like to unpredictable CMYK equivalents for printing. In the meantime, moiré patterns have a certain charm all of their own.

SPOT colour is the simplest and cheapest way of adding colour highlights to pages. It can be used in lots of ways, from picking out headings or rules to turning mono photos into subtle duotones. Spot colour is easy to apply and to control – just specify the shade you want, such as the colour of a company's logo as the spot colour for its company newsletter. Most DTP programs can cope with spot colour easily, but check that you have 'marked up' each item correctly and made the right things come out in colour.

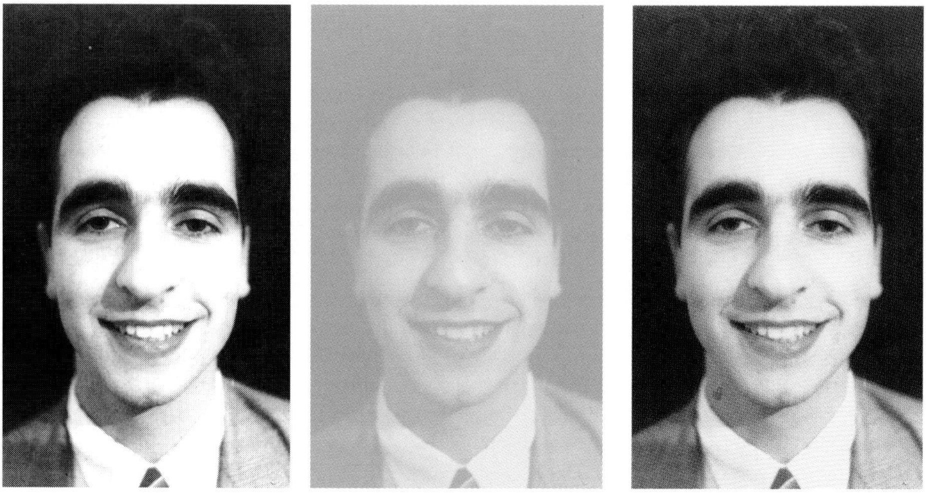

A duotone is a two-colour halftone, made from an ordinary black and white photo. The black plate is made more contrasty, and the second colour is flattened, to enhance mid-tones. The two different colours can have other differences – for instance using different screens on each colour – try changing the resolution or type of screen.

If you create logos or special graphics in a drawing program, you may want to lay a different colour underneath them in your page layout program. A problem that occurs on enclosed shapes is that people often layer a white filled shape on top of a black area. This is fine whilst your background is white, but will show up as soon as you change the colour of the background. To get around this, create shapes that are one long piece that curves around and overlaps, as illustrated in these letter 'O's.

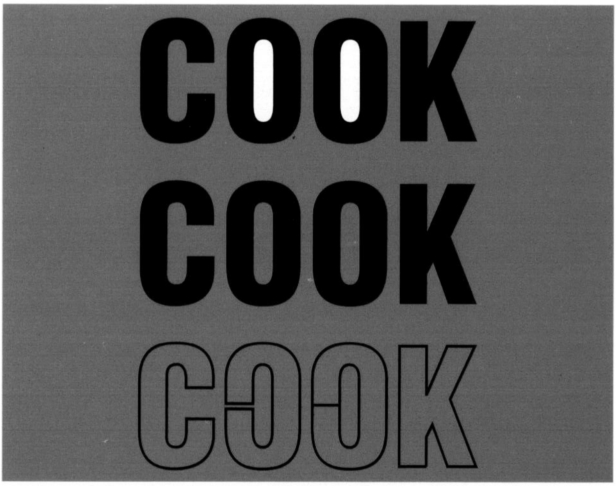

Trapped!

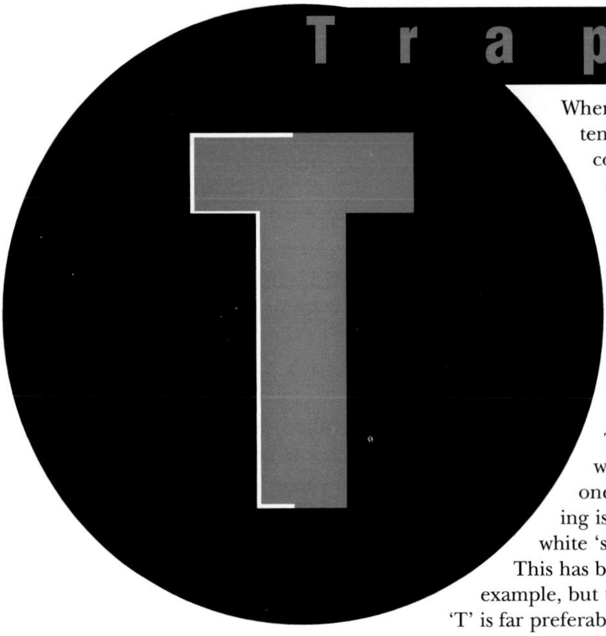

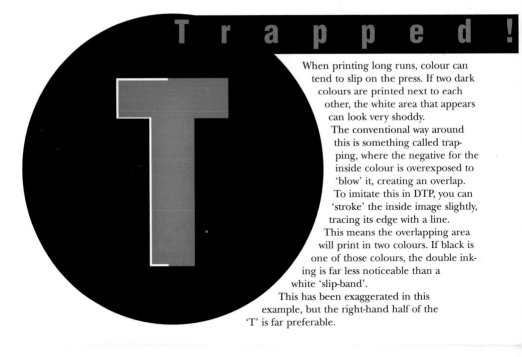

When printing long runs, colour can tend to slip on the press. If two dark colours are printed next to each other, the white area that appears can look very shoddy.

The conventional way around this is something called trapping, where the negative for the inside colour is overexposed to 'blow' it, creating an overlap.

To imitate this in DTP, you can 'stroke' the inside image slightly, tracing its edge with a line.

This means the overlapping area will print in two colours. If black is one of those colours, the double inking is far less noticeable than a white 'slip-band'.

This has been exaggerated in this example, but the right-hand half of the 'T' is far preferable.

Another way to avoid trapping problems is to print a solid of the colour showing through. On the right hand half of this circle, magenta has been printed solidly. Notice that this makes the black actually look more solid. This is standard practice in magazine printing to beef up the blacks.

The same has been done here – the left hand half of the circle is pure black ink, the right-hand side has solid yellow and solid black. This also avoids any chance of a white hairline due to printing mis-registration.

Of course in some instances it is impossible to overprint the second colour. When cyan is to print out of magenta, cyan *over*printing magenta gives a totally different colour.

"Runaround me" said the graphic to the text.
"Why should I go around you?" replied the text.

If you are incorporating graphics into a page-makeup program, use process colours in the graphic. That way when you print separations, anything tagged in, for instance, Cyan on the graphic will come out on the Cyan film of the made-up page. You can then print this film with whatever colour ink you want for your spot colour.

THE STANDARD way of adding full colour to pages often works uneasily with desktop systems, as computers calculate colour in different ways to colour imagesetters and printers. Traditional process colour uses the CMYK model to create real full-colour images in the final output; this breaks down images into quantities of the four colours Cyan (bright blue to people who aren't printers), Magenta (sort of red), Yelo (yellow), and Key (black), and then prints them in four passes to produce a glowing result.

Getting good colour has much to do with the skill of the repro house which creates the colour separations, as the four slices of colour image are called, even if you have specified the colours carefully. Even so you should try to get high-quality colour proofs such as cromalins to check that the final result bears more than a passing resemblance to your intentions. Checking negative films takes a lot of practice.

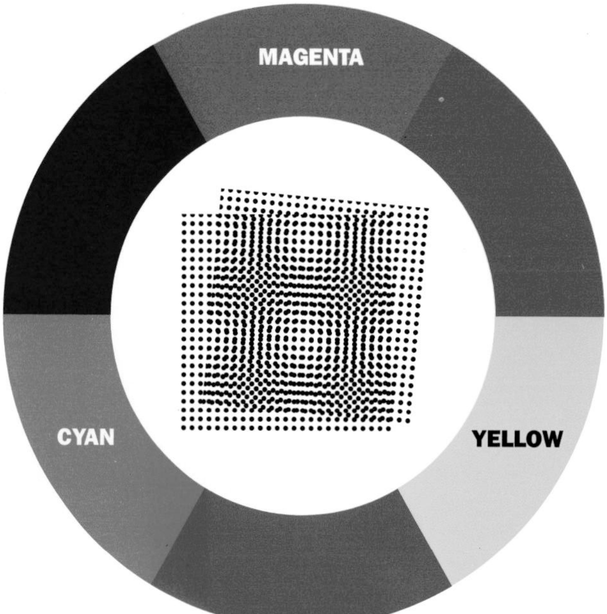

This colourwheel shows the colours obtained by mixing equal solids of the three basic process colours, Cyan Magenta and Yellow.
If possible, try and use a solid of one colour, with a tint of only one other colour.
This makes it impossible to get a moiré pattern.
The moiré pattern in the circle is an example of two screens meshed together at inappropriate angles.

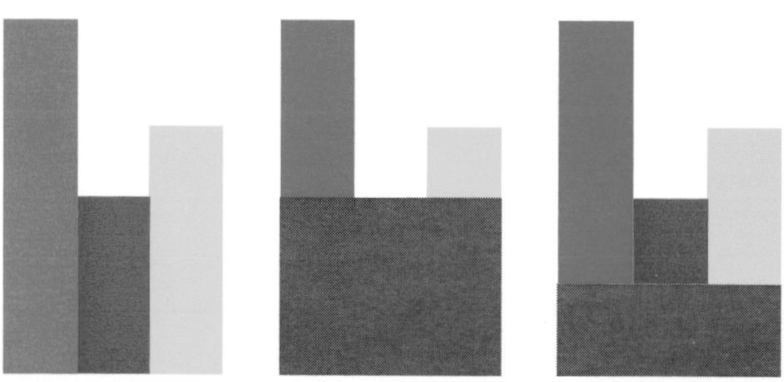

Four colour printing has trouble reproducing dark colours, because this requires a lot of ink. Too much ink on the press causes problems when printing.
One way around this is to make the assumption that equal amounts of all three process inks will produce grey, and to replace the process colours with an equal tint of black. This is called Grey Component Replacement, or GCR.

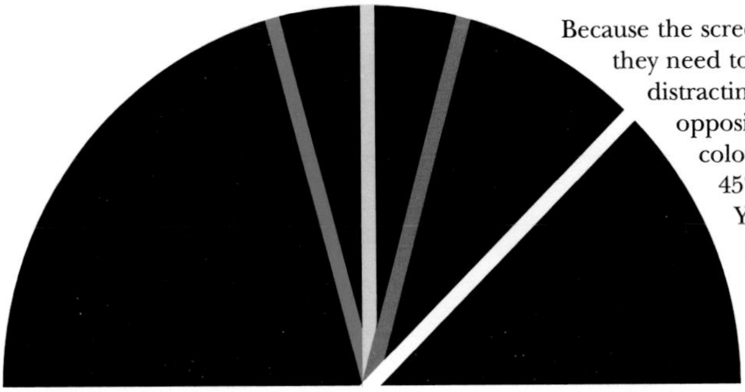

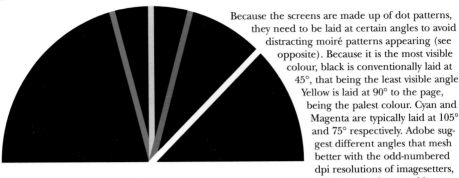

Because the screens are made up of dot patterns, they need to be laid at certain angles to avoid distracting moiré patterns appearing (see opposite). Because it is the most visible colour, black is conventionally laid at 45°, that being the least visible angle. Yellow is laid at 90° to the page, being the palest colour. Cyan and Magenta are typically laid at 105° and 75° respectively. Adobe suggest different angles that mesh better with the odd-numbered dpi resolutions of imagesetters, which are implemented by some applications.

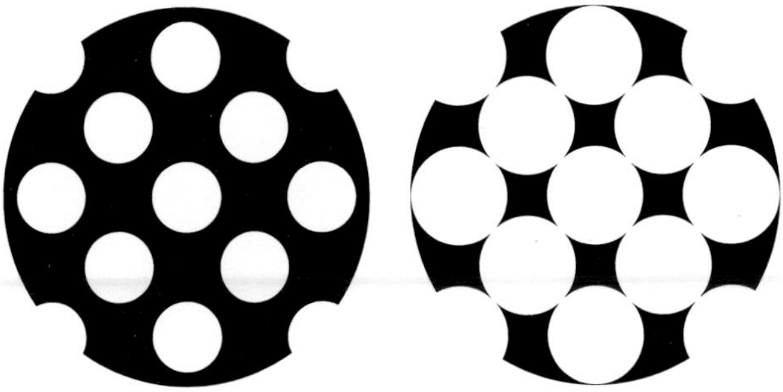

When a certain tone is reached, dots start to touch. When this happens, tones start to fill in as the area around the dots point of contact floods. Conventional separation systems use elliptical dots to avoid this.

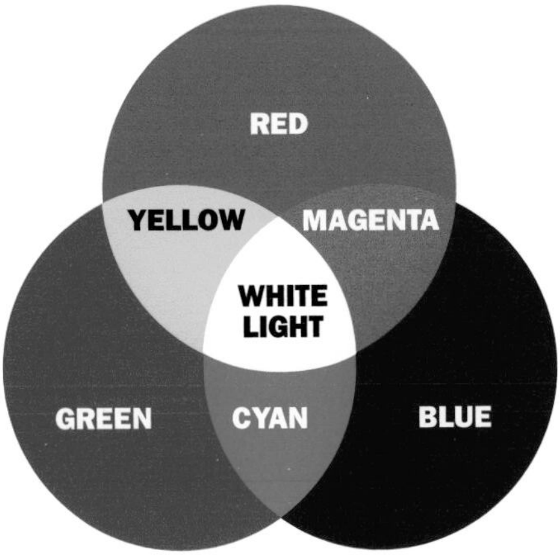

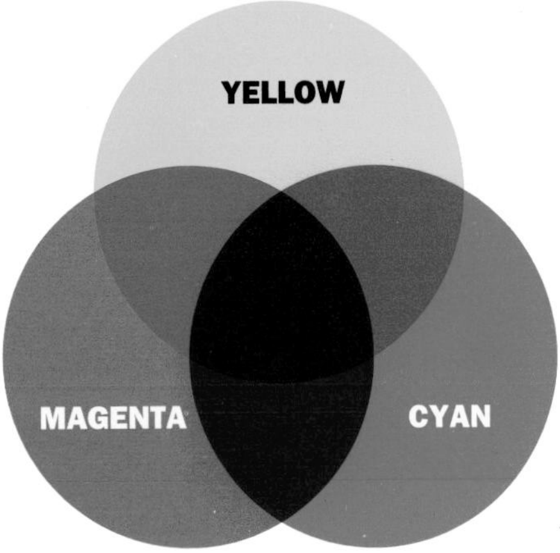

WYSIWYG, the famous "What You See is What You Get" doesn't hold true for colour. Your computer screen uses light to produce colour, and paper uses inks, so comparing what you see on screen with the final printed result is a bit like comparing minerals to vegetables.

Red, Green and Blue light can be combined to produce white light, and so this system is called 'additive colour'. Cyan, Magenta and Yellow colours are displayed by subtracting one of the additive primaries, and so this system is called subtractive colour. Alternatively known as RGB and CMYK colour models.

Because of these differences, some colours that look great on screen will look mushy when printed. Bright colours on screen are formed by blasting lots of light, but when printed they don't use enough ink to get decent coverage, and you tend to notice the dot screen used more than the actual colour!

DESKTOP COLOUR retouching programs are great creative tools. This is one of the major advantages of using your computer for colour repro – the creative opportunities. Once you've created an image on the computer you have two alternatives for output – producing a transparency or going straight to separated films.

This image was produced by sending the final image file to a slide bureau, and conventionally separating the slide.

This method incurs the cost of conventional colour separaration as well as the cost of having the slide produced, and introduces an extra process which would be skipped if separated films were produced direct from disk. However this is currently the most hassle-free way of getting a computer created image onto paper.

Separated films for this page were produced directly from the disk file on an ordinary Linotronic 300. This machine is not really designed for producing four-colour separations, but it is readily available, and demonstrates what can easily be done with desktop colour separation.

The image file was three megabytes, and took 30 minutes to process. Some bureaus will charge an hourly rate for their imagesetter, so producing separations this way can sometimes mount up to more than going the conventional route!

10 Document handling

WHEN computers first made it into the office a myth grew up that one day there would be a thing called the paperless office, work would be a tidy organised place with no scraps of paper to litter desks and get lost. Even now quite sophisticated computer users hold the most extraordinary beliefs about the power of the PC; that electronic documents, unlike paper ones, cannot get lost, that Apple Macintoshes are easy to use, and so on.

Collier's Rules

In the real world computers are just as messy as any other form of document production and need just as much organisation, if not more. If you lose a transparency or the copy for a feature in a paper-based studio, you can at least turn the place upside down till you find it. On the computer, unless you're well-prepared, it could be gone for ever.

Common sense organisation is the first step. Make sure that all files are stored in folders relating to each document or issue of a magazine, and that there is a backup copy of both text and illustrations on another storage device, whether it's a floppy disk or tape back-up system. Clearly label each stage through which the document travels, so that a colleague doesn't confuse your rough preliminary version with the finished thing and send the wrong file to the bureau.

Get to know your hardware and software thoroughly. Manuals are some of the most boring documents ever written, but reading these, relevant magazines and swapping tips with other users will mean that you are prepared for the day when nothing happens when you turn your computer on or you need to do something complicated with an illustration and your layout program won't do it. As well as design, layout, word processing and image manipulation software it's a good idea to have copies of utility programs to deal with computer viruses, lost files and broken disks, and to know how to use them. Relying solely on the office techie to help out in every emergency is a sure way to guarantee that she's not there when your hard disk dies and a deadline looms.

Other problems can be caused by incompatibilities between applications and even fonts. If you've just introduced a new program to your computer and mysterious mishaps have begun to occur, check out every program in turn, taking them off the computer and reinstalling them in turn to find out where the problem lies. Make a note of any known bugs in applications you use and recommended ways of working round them.

There are two main things which go wrong with fonts; they don't download to the printer correctly so your document is printed with the wrong fonts, or they don't print at all. The root problems are lack of memory and font clashes, caused by the somewhat ad hoc way computers recognise fonts.

While it's amazing that computers can store so much information in their memories it's less amazing when the memory falls over and loses the document you're working on. This is a particular problem for designers who tend to work with large files, as computers use lots of memory to store complicated visual information. The main remedy here is to check that there are no viruses affecting your computer and to save your work regularly so that any losses are minimised.

Even when you've sorted out all the production difficulties at your end, if you're using a bureau for final output there's plenty that can go wrong right up to the creation of your film. To start with make sure that you send the bureau the right version of the file, and that you've followed their guidelines on image file formats and so on. The bureau will need to know exactly which fonts you are using as it needs to duplicate your work using the exact same ones, and which versions of application software you're using.

Whether you're sending files to the bureau on disk or by modem, make sure that the bureau knows what to expect. Fax over a list of file names, including details of document length and type of document. That way if half a file gets lost or corrupted somewhere along the way, you can find out at once and send it again.

Always check the film when you receive it, especially graphics such as tables or charts. Blobs and other special characters are particularly prone to disappearing completely during the production process.

Above all remember that electronic design and publishing is very much a developing art. Little of the equipment available to you is perfect and most of it is in a continuous state of improvement. The best you can do is to be careful, well-organised, and insured against the inevitable disasters through good planning.

16/ Proofreader's marks

JUST WHEN you thought everything was safely on-screen and you could say hello to the paperless studio, it's time to remember the traditional paper-based proof-reader's marks. It remains good practice to produce and carefully examine at least one paper proof – it's surprising how many mistakes can be picked up by doing this – and studying the range of marks gives a good indication of the type of mistakes which can easily occur.

meaning	**marginal marks**	**in text**
marks of instruction		
correction is concluded	/	none
leave unchanged	stet	the copy must be changed
query	(?)	who's copy must be changed
broken letter	(x)	the copy must be changed
wrong font	w.f.	*the copy must be changed*
spell it out	sp	12 proofs were sent to her
correct vertical alignment		The copy must be changed What are they?
remove extraneous marks	(x)	
deletion, insertion, substitution		
insert space	#	The copy must not be changed
insert characters	λp	The co y must be changed
close up		Let's c hange the copy
delete		Why not change the copy/

meaning	**marginal marks**	**in text**
deletion, insertion, substitution		
delete and close up	⁀₰‿	Th~~h~~e copy will be changed
multiple corrections	⁀₰‿ / ⋏l /	Th~~h~~e copy wi/ be changed
equalize spacing	eq #	The ⋏ copy must be ⋏ changed
indent 1 em		□The copy has been changed
indent 2 ems		□□The copy was changed
move left	4mm	[the copy must be changed
move right	2mm	] the copy must be changed
raise	1·5mm	⌐the copy must be changed¬
lower	2mm	the copy must be changed ⌙___⌟
add leading	ld	>the copy must be changed the copy must be changed
substitute character	⋏ will	the copy ~~must~~ be changed
punctuation		
period	⊙	change the copy ⋏
comma	,	change the copy⋏he said
semi-colon	;	he sent the copy⋏
colon	(:)	first⋏change the copy
apostrophe	ˇ'ˇ	don⋏t change the copy
exclamation	!	change the copy⋏

meaning	marginal marks	in text
punctuation		
hyphen	=	we are copyediting
en dash	/–/	3694
em dash	1/m	the copy with corrections
brackets	(/)	it the copy must not be changed
superior figures	2	242
inferior figures	2	CO2
substitute ligature	fl	florence
insert oblique	(/)	0802
open and close quotes	" "	don't change the copy, he said
question mark	?	shall I change the copy
type styles		
lower-case	lc	THE TYPE STYLE OF THIS COPY
capitals	caps	the type style of this copy
small capitals	sm caps	the copy is being changed
capitals and small capitals	caps & s.c.	it is being changed again
upper and lower-case	u&lc	this is all lower-case copy

meaning	marginal marks	in text
type styles		
roman	rom	this is not *roman*
italic	ital	this copy must change
boldface	bf	the copy has changed
boldface italic	bf ital	or has it?
position marks and paragraph		
begin a paragraph	¶	the end. A new beginning
no paragraph	no ¶	end. The next paragraph was
transpose letters	tr	the copy has been checked
transpose words	tr	the copy been has checked
transpose lines	tr	secondly, the copy firstly, the idea
transpose a number of lines	3 1 2	the third line the first line the second line
centre	[ ]	[this copy is ranged left]
response to query		
correct as set	ok	the copy was changed twice
OK with corrections	ok w/c	the copy was changed 2 times

DTP is particularly useful for simplifying repeat jobs. Once a style has been set, templates can be created which give a rough outline to the page, and all the typestyles used can be listed by function rather than having to select name, size and style each time. Templates can also ensure consistency of design; some DTP programs, such as Interleaf, FrameMaker and Ventura Publisher, are intended to make this particularly easy, while others such as Quark XPress and Design Studio, place more emphasis on the creative role of the designer.

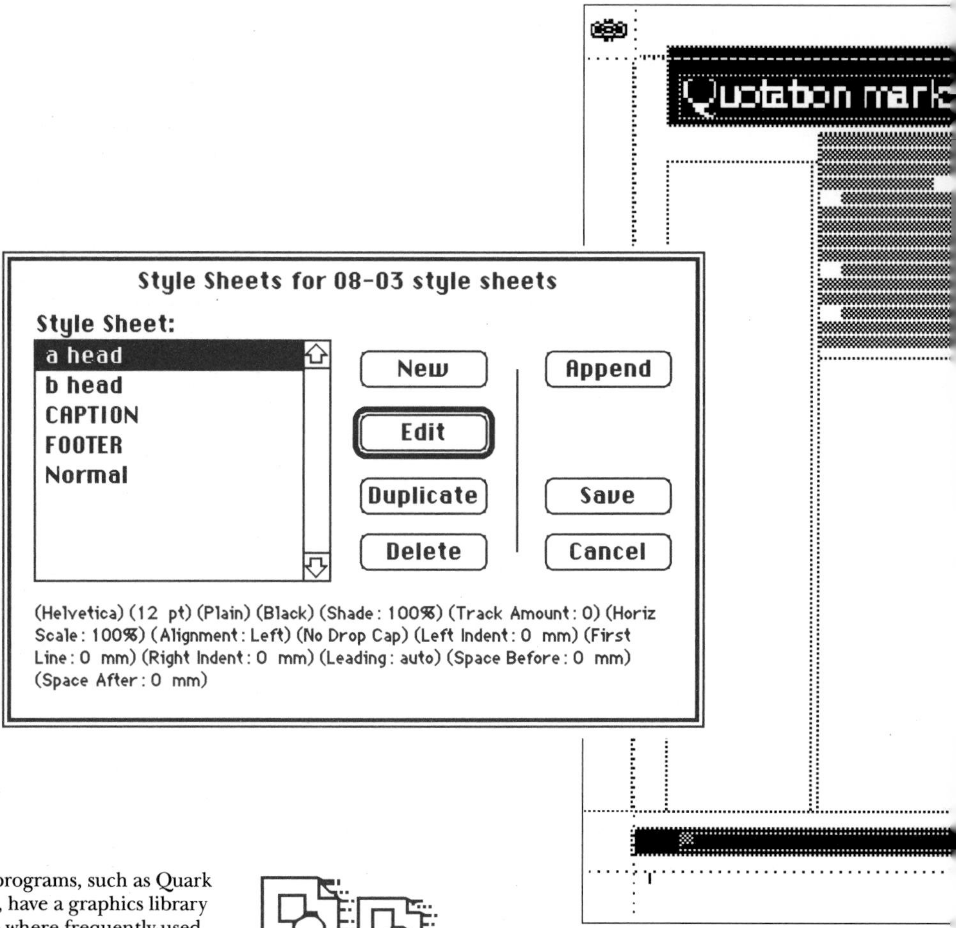

Some programs, such as Quark XPress, have a graphics library feature where frequently-used graphics can be stored ready for use. Even if your program doesn't have such a feature it's a good idea to keep graphics in a safe place on your hard disk with back-up copies to hand.

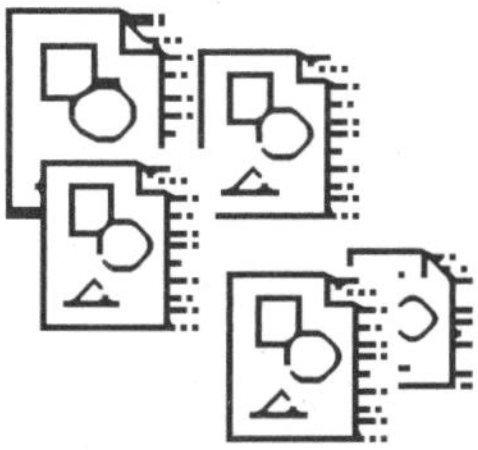

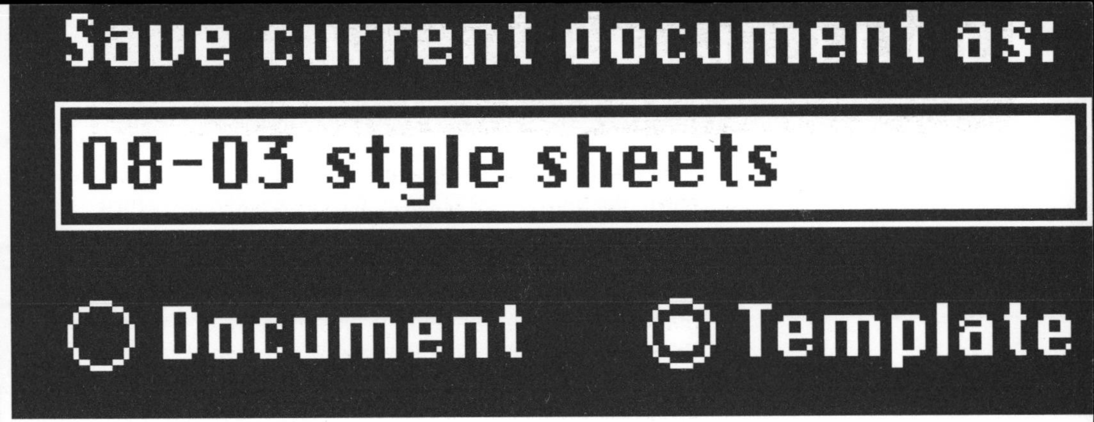

Standardise heading sizes or options for body copy with a style sheet in the form of a menu. As well as saving time this means that everyone will stick to the style, even freelancers unfamiliar with it.

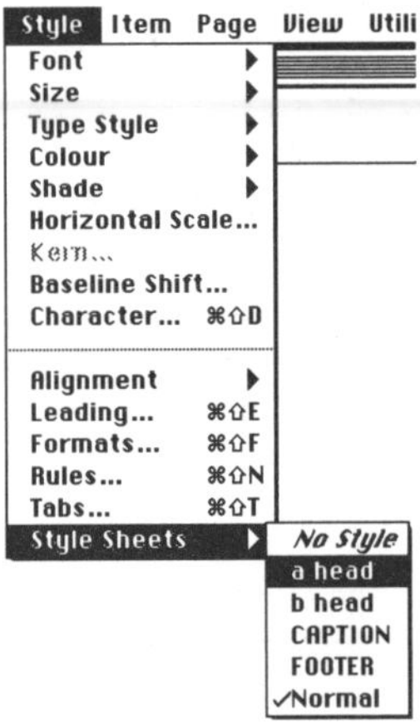

Where many similar documents are to be produced from one initial design, it is useful to set up a template document. Each new document then created from the template will follow the same style automatically.

For documents with many repeated pages, it may be worth using a DTP program which works on the basis of master, or default, pages. Only the first example of the page needs to be designed, and then copy and illustrations can be flowed on to the page simply and quickly. This approach works well for technical documentation, where designers will probably only be used to work on the initial concept.

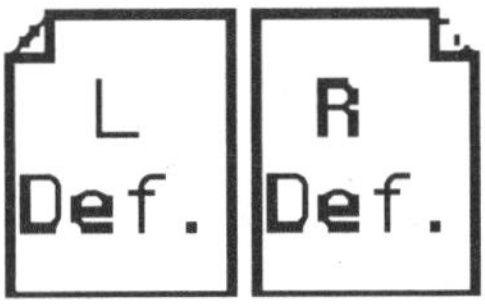

10/4 Document handling

GOOD design and typography will only take you halfway to the successful creation of documents. Good organisation is necessary to ensure that the deadline is met, that time is not wasted by files getting lost, virus attacks, computer networks breaking down or someone not having the right version of PageMaker. The more people working on a project, the better the organisation needs to be.

Establish a schedule of tasks and deadlines and make sure everyone on the team knows about it and sticks to it, and make sure that back-up copies of both applications and text and picture files are always to hand. Immutable laws of publishing decree that the day you don't stick to these rules is the day when your hard disk will crash, taking three weeks' work with it.

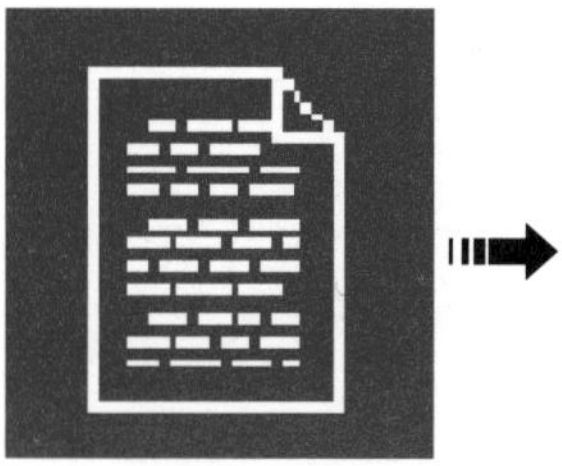

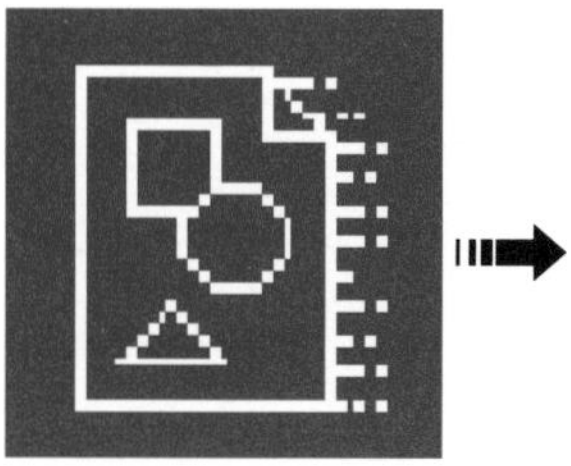

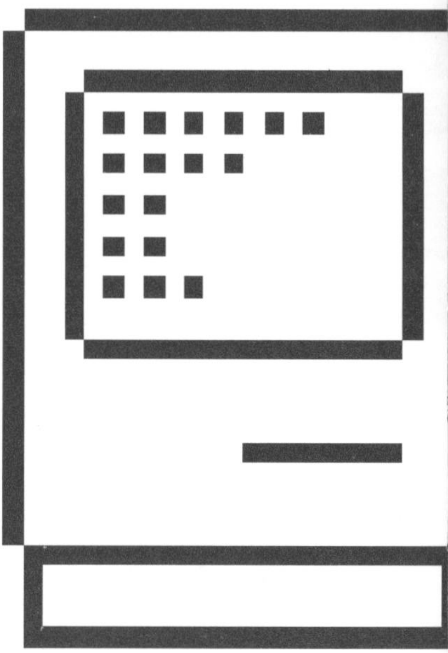

Ensure that all writers have a copy of the style guide if there is one, and submit text in the chosen format (eg Word 4.0, WordPerfect 5.1) and on disks which your computers can read.

Save time by using search and replace to correct punctuation (eg double spaces after full stops) and recurrent spelling or style errors (eg color for colour).

Don't rely on spellcheckers to pick up every mistake – they don't spot correctly-spelt but wrongly-chosen words.

Establish a standard format for graphics and illustrations, which your software and hardware can cope with.

Keep standard graphic elements such as logos in a library.

Keep transparencies and prints firmly and clearly labelled and stored so they don't get lost when it's time for the page to go to the linotronic bureau.

Make sure every workstation has the same version of your page make-up program, the same fonts and the same style sheets.

Give each layout a distinct name and don't let anyone work on the back-up copy.

Designers and editors should liaise to make sure that nothing important is left out and that any necessary changes, eg cuts to copy, are made.

If you're working on a network or accepting a lot of floppy disks from outside contributors, install a virus checker.

Save work regularly.

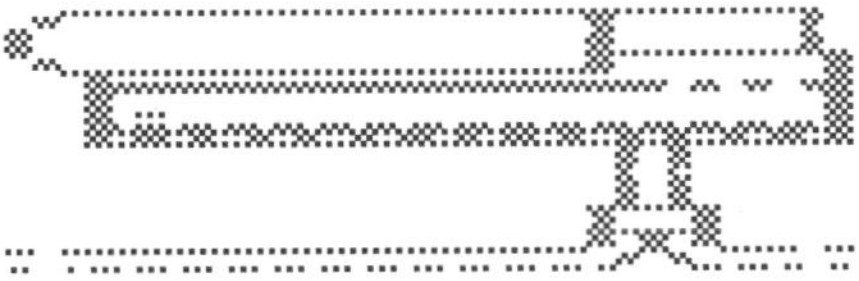

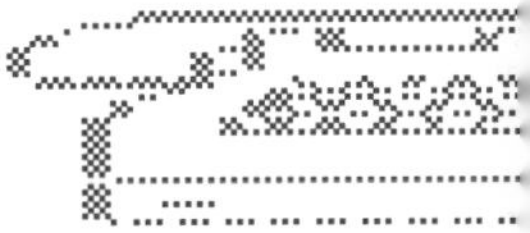

Unless you are using an expensive and sophisticated publishing system, you will need to rely on a paper or dry-wipe board progress chart to make sure that all jobs are being done on time. This allows you to spot areas which are lagging behind and do something about it.

It's also a good idea to keep phone numbers of useful people – support desks, consultants, your bureau, writers and illustrators – in paper form rather than on the computer which will have lost them or broken down when you need them.

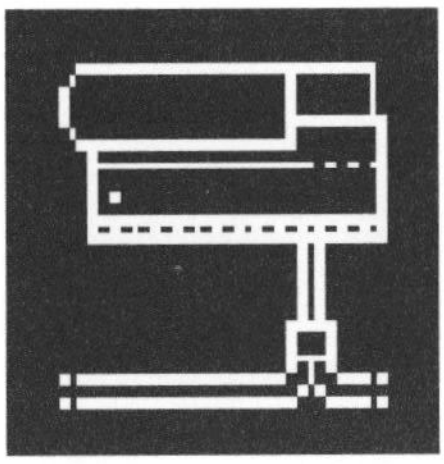

Produce a paper proof to show the boss and to check how the page really looks.

Don't try to correct small type on reduced size proofs; print the page in tiles or work on screen.

Make sure that all the fonts are available to the printer, or it will substitute standard typefaces and produce something which looks nothing like what you intended.

Make sure that all interested parties are satisfied with the page.

Collect the page layout file and any other material (additional fonts, graphics, etc) in a folder. Even if a graphic has been added to the page some bureaux like a copy of the original file for safety.

Enclose a print-out of the layout with any additional instructions, such as colour mark-up, clearly indicated.

However you send your files to your bureau, make sure that you keep copies of everything which has gone.

Liaise with the bureau staff to make sure that they have received everything you think you have sent, and that they know what to do with it. Both bikes and modems can mysteriously lose files...

Keep a copy of order forms so that you don't pay for their mistakes.

CHOOSING and working happily with an output bureau can make all the difference to your work. Most of the problems which happen with DTP happen at this final stage, as files are transferred to and output from a totally different piece of equipment, the imagesetter. When DTP consisted of single colour text and line illustrations, there was less to go wrong but now that many users are creating and separating full-colour continuous tone artwork on their desktop computers, there is much more room for error.

Choose a bureau that can satisfy your demands. Don't go to the cheapest if it cannot handle the volume of work or the speed of turn-around you need. If you are doing colour work, check that the operators at the bureau understand your requirements and know about colour planning; it is a skill, and with much of the software still in early stages of development there is plenty that can go wrong. A bureau which invests in skilled, well-trained staff could save you money compared to a cheaper operation with less-skilled staff who mess up your documents and cause you to miss important deadlines.

StuffIt 1.5.1

If you're sending files to the bureau by modem, make sure they know what files to expect and check that all of the files have arrived in one piece.

The imagesetting bureau proofs their runout against your laser proof – without this there is no easy way of spotting problems before they get back to you.

If you don't specify whether or not you require the crop marks to print, the imagesetting bureau will probably print according to the last instructions in your print dialogue box – an easy mistake to make but potentially very annoying and expensive.

Your document can be output onto bromide or film. If you are outputting onto film, instruct your imagesetting bureau as to the type of film required by your printer *(see ch. 8)*.

If you are producing artwork for colour printing, specify separated artwork if necessary.

Make sure that you haven't accidentally picked the wrong colours – an easy mistake to make in PageMaker, especially if you're using a mono screen, but an expensive one to put right if you only find out when the film comes back.

If graphics and artwork are being incorporated into made-up pages, send the bureau copies of the original graphic file as well as the version on the page or the encapsulated PostScript file (EPSF). This helps the bureau if there are any problems.

File name	10-05 Linotronic tips
Program used	QuarkXPress 3
Fonts used	New baskerville, M Gill sans
Imported graphics	None
Laser proof supplied?	Yes
Page size	A4
Reduction/enlargement	100%
Crop marks	No
Screen frequency (lpi)	133
Screen orientation (degrees)	45
No of pages to print	1
Output	Bromide
Separations	black and cyan

It is important to supply the version number of the program.

Check that your bureau has copies of the same software and fonts you are planning to use, and that the fonts are from the same designer – one Garamond can bear very little resemblance to another, and if the widths don't match, your document could be ruined.

If your bureau tells you that one form of file format outputs more quickly, standardise on it. Some users find that TIFF files output more quickly than PICTs.

Make sure that you specify this – especially if you have been proofing at a reduced size on your laser printer – otherwise the bureau will print your document at the size specified in your page setup dialogue box.

The screen frequency and screen orientation define the look of the tints on your prints. The higher the frequency, the smaller the dots (or thinner the lines) used to represent tints. The higher the frequency, the larger the range of tones that can be printed.

You can change the angle that the screen is printed at by changing the orientation.

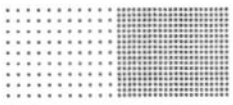

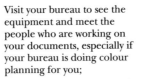

Visit your bureau to see the equipment and meet the people who are working on your documents, especially if your bureau is doing colour planning for you; it's interesting to see the equipment and it will improve everyone's understanding of what you want done with your documents.

11 Hypermedia

LOOK AT THESE PAGES. Suppose I said **'HyperText'**. If you wanted to know what that meant, you'd have to grudgingly turn to the glossary, search for the word and read the explanation, then flick back and find where you'd just left off. Boring. Imagine if you could just click on that word and immediately its definition would pop up, along with a descriptive picture, and perhaps a spoken description or an animation. Well, it's happening today, and it's called hypermedia.

A hypermedia system, like print media, is simply a way of storing and accessing information, except, in this instance, the information is stored on a computer, and is read or viewed by its audience on a screen. By using the computer as a medium, hypermedia allows extra dimensions to the ways information can be accessed and presented.

Firstly, it allows many types of media to be used. In a book, there are two basic components of design – text and graphics – whether they be photographs or illustrations. Hypermedia opens up the possibility of adding sound, computer animation and moving video to this list.

Computers can now read from compact discs, which can store large amounts of data, enough to combine video, animation, sound, graphics and text onto a single disc. In future, products that combine some or all of these media will be commonplace in the office and the home.

Hypermedia also allows a whole new set of ways that the audience can interact with information. These provide new and powerful means of allowing the user to find and manipulate related information.

All examples used in this chapter are from work done by DeCode Design.

In a printed book, we use a set of established mechanisms to help the reader find and use the contained information, such as contents pages and glossaries. Hypermedia's database facilities add to this the ability to search for and sort information, and the means to automate the work of transporting the user between two or more bits of related content.

The design of hypermedia presents major new challenges few have faced before. One issue is finding ways to harness the full potential of combining so many forms of media. While this presents fantastic new creative possibilities, there is the risk of overloading the audience with information, and allowing the form of the information to become more important than the content.

The second major challenge of hypermedia design is using the interactive abilities of the computer in the most useful ways. Given the possibility to inter-relate all the content of a production, a task well beyond even the most grandiose budgets, we have to face a set of decisions about what are the most important and meaningful ways of connecting the discrete aspects of the information presented. While many of these choices may appear obvious, predicting the audience's desires opens up a veritable can of worms.

In this brief exploration of hypermedia, we are not afforded the ability to look at all the different systems that can be used for its creation or use, but then that's not really the point. Whatever the system, the design issues encountered will be the same.

At the heart of the dilemma facing designers in this new territory is providing the audience with simple and intuitive ways of using their system, without losing the magical possibilities that the medium presents. While everyone knows how to 'use' a book or magazine, the same is not true for the current generation of computers.

In the same way, there is a need to provide a set of standard means for structuring a hypermedia 'book' so its audience doesn't have to learn from scratch how to use each new system. This is the most important aspect of the information presented here. The following pages outline a set of standard devices that hypermedia designers can use to ensure that their productions are as easy to use as possible. Just as the rest of this book outlines a clear and easy to follow set of guidelines to help you make effective use of the computer as a design tool, so here we provide clear guidelines on hypermedia design. Clear ideas apply to any system – the concepts discussed for ordering information are equally applicable to print design.

HYPERMEDIA, or multimedia as it is more commonly known, is essentially the ability to mix sound, vision and data into an interactive program used on a computer. It is possible to use and produce hypermedia on a standard office personal computer and it has many business applications. The potential market for hypermedia products is set to explode in the 90s with the emergence of a new class of computer designed specifically for multimedia. These take the form of self-contained players designed primarily for domestic use.

CD ROM-XA

Compact disc, read only memory, extended architecture (CD ROM-XA) is supported by both Sony and computer software giant Microsoft. It is designed as a means of upgrading the standard office personal computer to be able to access hypermedia products that combine animation, CD quality sound, text and low frame rate small screen video.

DVI

Digital Video Interactive (DVI) is the first system available for the integration of full-motion video into personal computer applications. Developed initially by RCA, and now owned by Intel and supported by IBM, it is primarily designed as a means of upgrading the standard IBM compatible personal computer to include the ability to playback digital video from the computer's hard disk or a CD ROM drive.

Video

Increasingly multimedia systems are able to integrate full-screen full-motion video, as simply another type of data the computer can handle. The hardware necessary to handle video will soon be cheap enough to include in every personal computer.

Data

A compact disc can store vast amounts of alpha-numeric data, all of which can be held in a database the user can easily search. The addition of audio and visual presentation techniques to large databases is the cornerstone of hypermedia potential.

Audio

Most of the new multimedia formats are based on an extension of the compact disc audio format, making use of large amounts of sound (either music, speech or sound effects) possible in an interactive product.

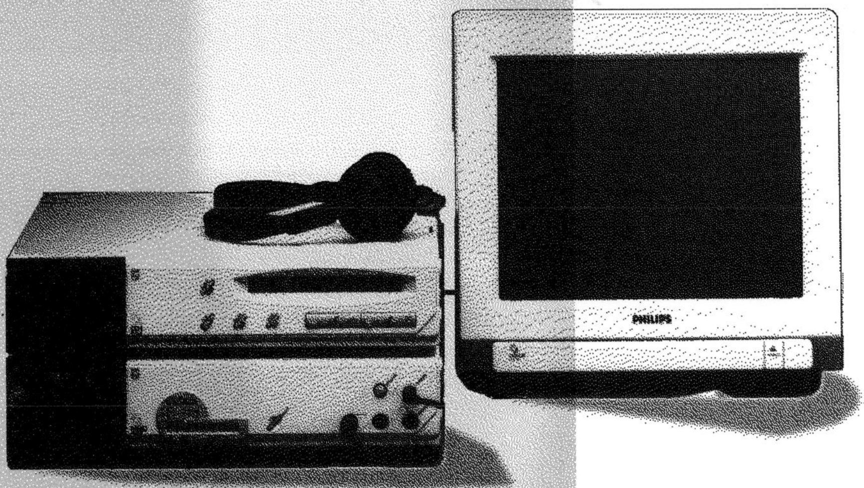

CDTV
Commodore Dynamic Total Vision (CDTV) is the first mass market multimedia player available for the home. Developed and marketed by Commodore, and based on the popular Amiga home computer, the first version of the machine does not support full-motion video, but this is promised with subsequent upgrades.

CD-I
Compact Disc Interactive (CD-I) is an extension of the existing world standard for compact disc audio. Supported by many of the world's major consumer electronics companies as a standard for sound, data and visuals on a single compact disc, it promises to provide a ubiquitous format for the distribution of multimedia information. CD-I players, which connect to both the TV, for play-back of the visual components, and to the stereo system, for high quality sound, are already available for commercial applications, and machines for the home will be available by 1992.

Graphics
To varying degrees all multimedia systems include the ability to display high resolution images and computer animation; both are powerful visual tools for embellishing the presentation of information or simulating processes.

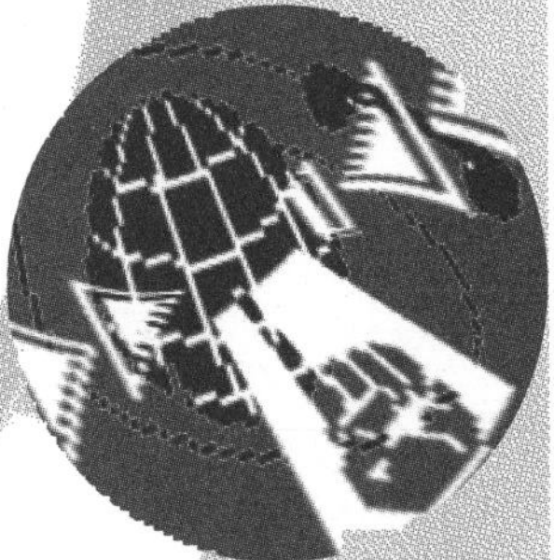

Interaction
The most important aspect of hypermedia is that it allows the user to interact with all the different types of information being presented, and to manipulate this data in many ways. This usurps the linearity of traditional communications media, such as print and TV.

INTERACTION is the key to multimedia. While the rules contained in this book about design will be useful when you come to developing a hypermedia system, the challenge is to use the interactive power of the computer in the most useful way, allowing the user to jump effortlessly between associated information.

A hypermedia data base is made up of screens of information, variously known as pages or cards. The analogy of a page is used, as the screens are often similar in design to the pages of a book, except that with hypermedia the pages are not read in a linear sequence. In fact each 'page' can provide the user with a huge choice of which page to access next. Collections of cards or pages are referred to as stacks or books.

Titles
The title icon tells the user their present location in the data base, and can be used to move backwards through the data base along the path used to reach the current point.

Directories
Clicking on A-Z will bring up a menu of all the artists listed in the database so the user can directly jump from *Arnolfini* to *Zebbedee,* avoiding *Machiavelli.*

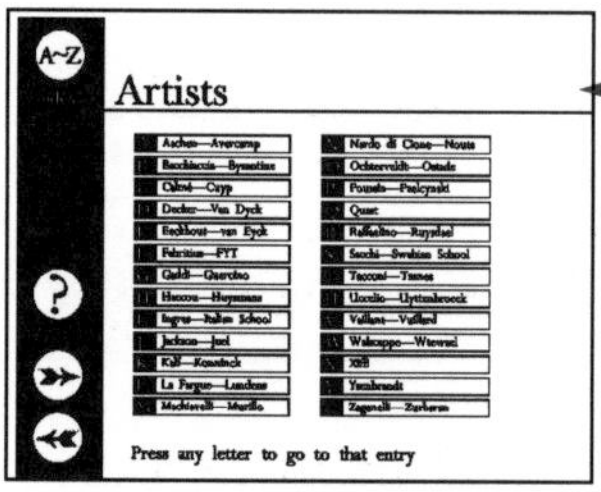

Searches
The question mark button allows the user to bring up a dialogue box to search the database for a reference to any word. So from *Da Vinci* you could search for all references to *Helicopter.*

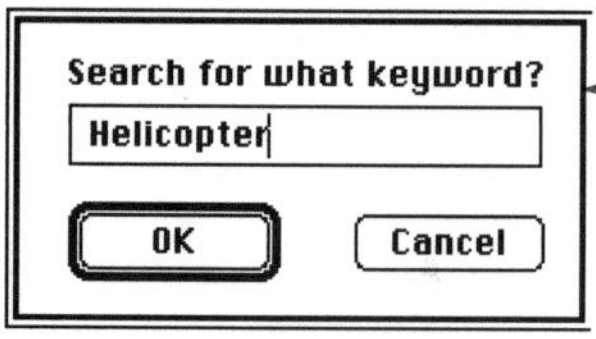

Local navigation
To simply move laterally to the next page of related information, the user selects the arrows facing left or right.

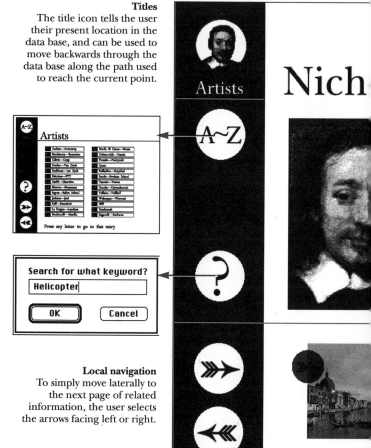

Navigation
In this example, the screen design contains a number of different ways of moving around the database. Going up and down the 'tree' of information is called a 'global' move. Left and right navigation between directly related pieces of information is called 'local' navigation.

So for instance moving from a page on *Da Vinci* to a page on the *Mona Lisa* is global navigation, because you are looking at different types of information (painter and painting). But moving from a page on the *Mona Lisa* to a page on the *Last Supper* would be local navigation, because both elements are the same type of data.

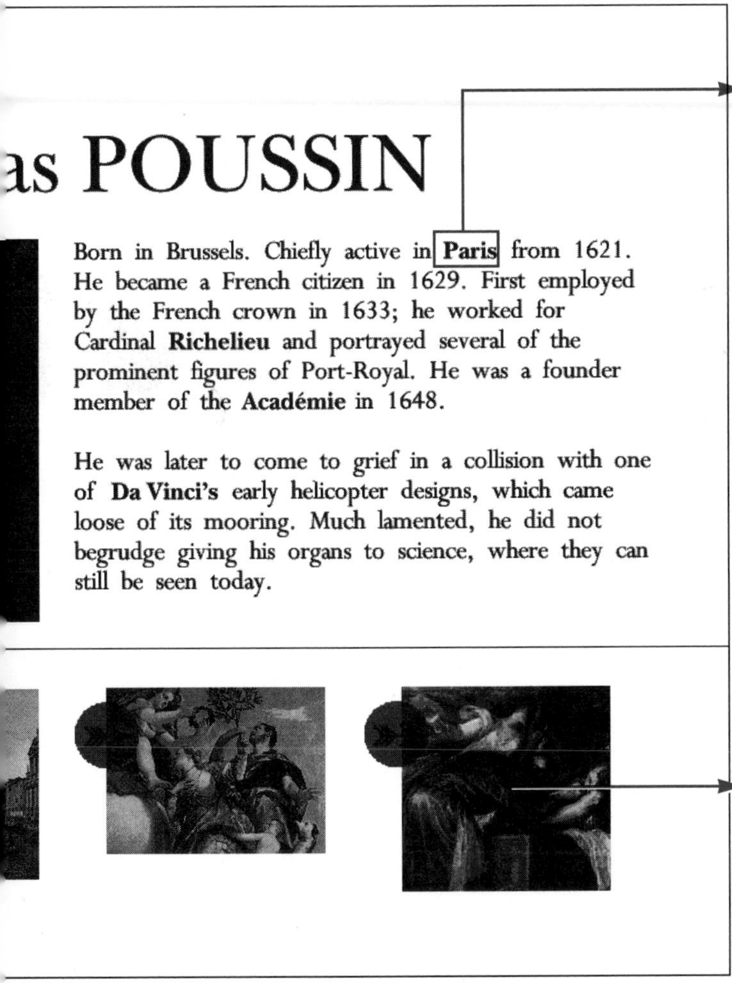

as POUSSIN
Born in Brussels. Chiefly active in **Paris** from 1621. He became a French citizen in 1629. First employed by the French crown in 1633; he worked for Cardinal **Richelieu** and portrayed several of the prominent figures of Port-Royal. He was a founder member of the **Académie** in 1648.
He was later to come to grief in a collision with one of **Da Vinci's** early helicopter designs, which came loose of its mooring. Much lamented, he did not begrudge giving his organs to science, where they can still be seen today.

Hot text
Words are bolded in the text to indicate to the user that there is a further reference in the database to that word. Clicking on one of them will take the user to that reference instantly, allowing access to associated data. This encourages the user to further explore a specific topic that most interests them.

Hot graphics
Selecting one of the thumbnail paintings displayed at the bottom of the page allows the user to get further information on each of the artist's paintings held in the database. These are known as graphic buttons, or 'hot graphics'.

THERE are many possible ways to design the links between the different pages of information in a hypermedia database. One of the most important issues for hypermedia design is providing the user with easy to understand ways to move through the information presented, which allow them to harness the associative powers of the medium while inside an intuitive framework. Here we look at some of the most common navigation concepts that can be employed, using the example of an interactive fashion catalogue.

Selecting *What's New* begins a video program that briefly introduces new fashions. Here the user can pause the video at any point and click on the screen to jump to details of any item of clothing presented in the sequence.

Title Pages
This is the first page that the user sees. It is much like the contents page of a book or a magazine. Here they can select between the different topics covered in the database.

Selecting *Sportswear* takes the user to this card which allows them to choose the specific area of sportswear that they are interested in.

Selecting *Jackets* takes the user to the first page on this type of garment. The left and right facing arrows are local navigational tools which move back and forward through all the sportswear jacket cards in the system, while the upward facing arrow moves back up the the tree structure to allow another sub-category of sportswear to be selected. More information on this particular item is available by using one of the icons on the bottom of the page.

From the running jacket page, the user can also go 'deeper' into the system and get more information on the garment. Here the user has the option of completing an order form, or looking at the jacket in a range of colours. The icon in the top left of every card returns to the title card, providing an easy way out of the system.

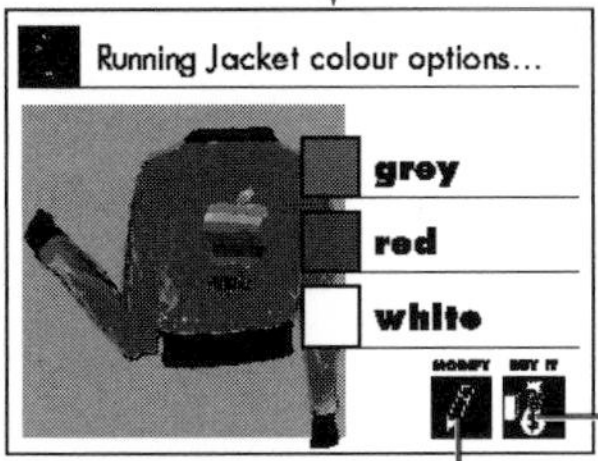

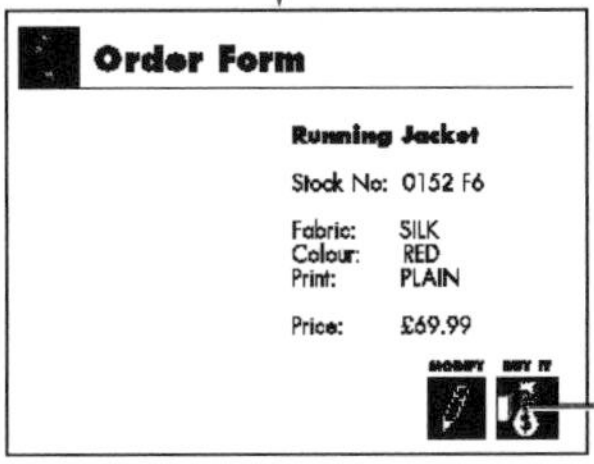

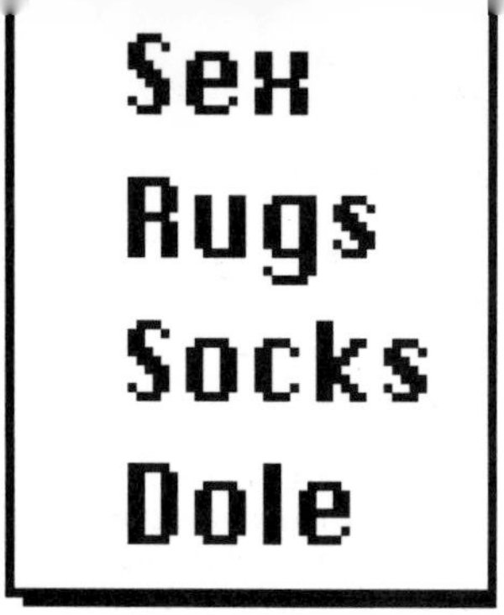

IN PRINT design there are a number of standard building blocks which can be employed in the presentation of information; primarily text and images, and classes of these such as captions and headlines. All of these will be useful in hypermedia design, but here there is the added dimension of interactivity. It is necessary to introduce new design concepts to control how the user moves around and navigates through the document. Some of the basic types of interactive control are explained below.

Menus
Customised menus give the user a series of choices. Most modern computer interfaces use pull down menus, which appear on the top of the screen when the user selects the menu title.

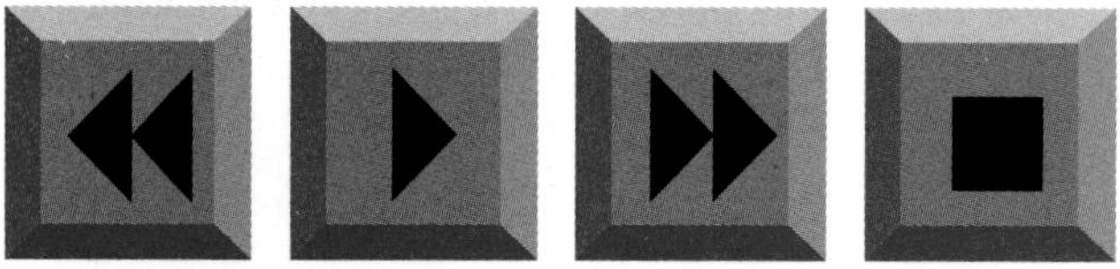

Buttons
The main means of interaction is through buttons, active areas of the screen that allow the user to move from one page display to another by clicking on them. Buttons are often referred to as icons, as a standard means of displaying them is to use a pictorial representation of what they do. The function of each icon should be standardised throughout a product.

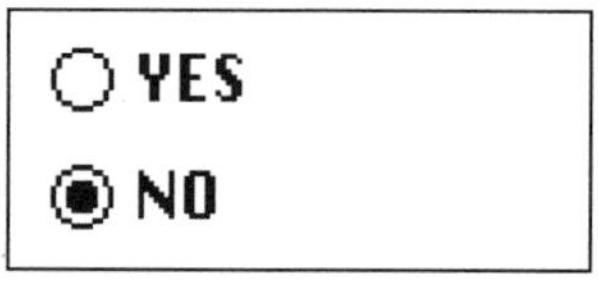

Radio buttons and check boxes
Interface design has developed its own syntax. Much like you use italics for a certain purpose in typesetting, so certain types of buttons are used in certain specific conditions; Radio buttons, like those on the right above, are used to make mutually exclusive choices. Therefore when one option is selected the other becomes deselected. Check buttons allow the selection of a number of complementary options.

User input

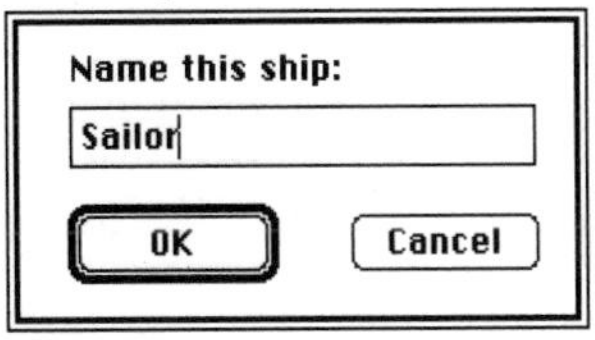
Name this ship:
Sailor
OK
Cancel

Alert

Sorry Man,
I've crashed
Finder

User option

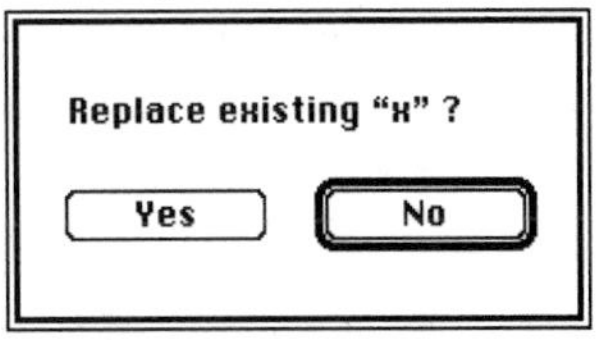
Replace existing "x" ?
Yes
No

Dialogue boxes
These have a number of applications. One is where a menu item needs further choices, or specific data to be entered, before the action can be carried out. Their other use is where there is a need to warn the user of the effects of the selection they have just made and to have it confirmed. This is particularly important where the action will irreparably change the system, such as deleting pages.

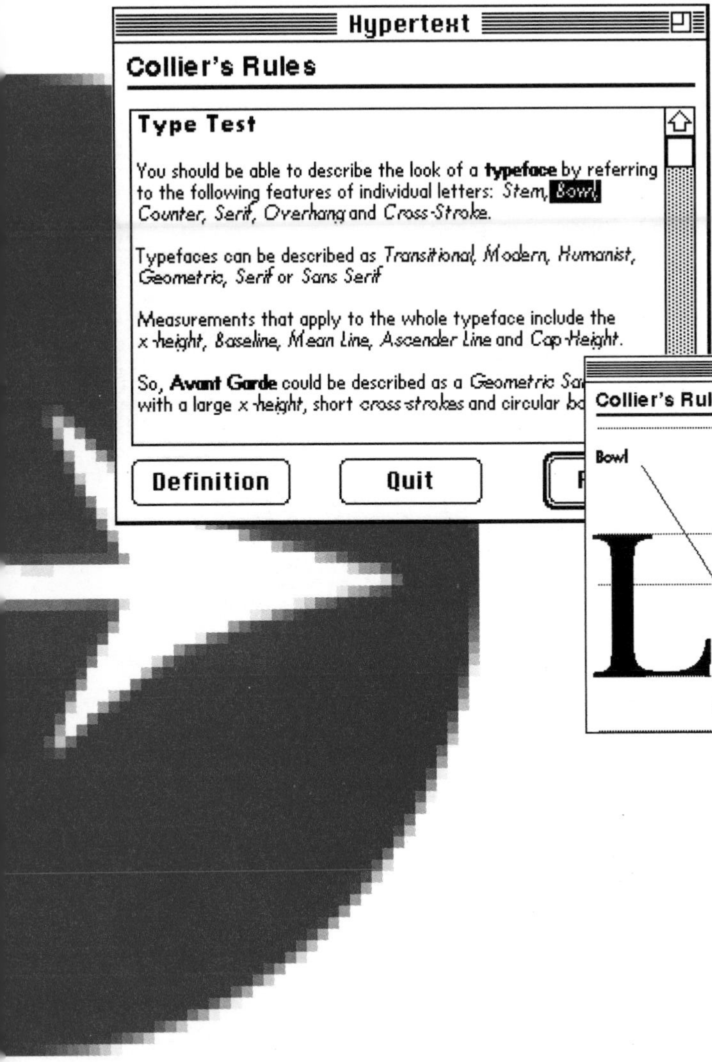
Hypertext
Collier's Rules
Type Test
You should be able to describe the look of a typeface by referring to the following features of individual letters: Stem, Bowl, Counter, Serif, Overhang and Cross-Stroke.
Typefaces can be described as Transitional, Modern, Humanist, Geometric, Serif or Sans Serif
Measurements that apply to the whole typeface include the x-height, Baseline, Mean Line, Ascender Line and Cap-Height.
Definition
Quit

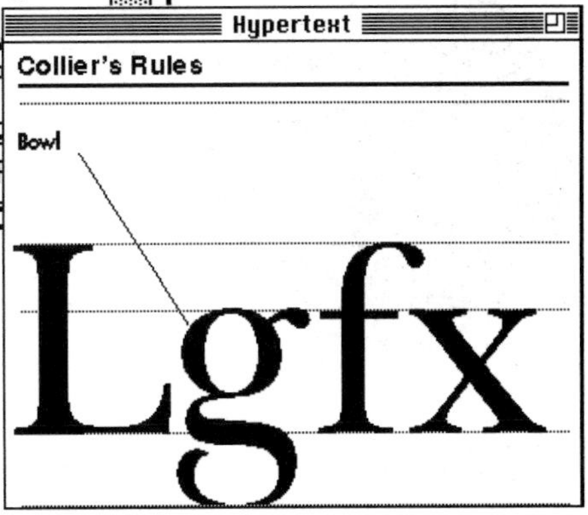
Hypertext
Collier's Rules
Bowl
Lgfx

Hot text
One standard device for interactivity is to turn a word into a button. An example of the effective use of hot text is in providing access to a glossary of terms. Here each word that appears in the glossary can be **bolded** when it appears in a page design, indicating to the user that clicking on it will automatically take them to its definition.

HYPERMEDIA'S DISTINCTION from other types of computer applications is that it integrates not only text and graphics, but also animation, sound, and increasingly video footage. This creates new challenges in the design of computer user interfaces. New metaphors and control techniques need to be devised which are as immediately understandable as possible. Just like good punctuation, a good interface should be invisible – so easy to use, you just go ahead without noticing.

User feedback
Interactive systems need to give their users constant feedback so that they are always aware of what is happening. A method of doing this is to design the system so that the visual representation of the cursor changes when it moves over an active zone. Alternatively audio cues can indicate when an error is made or when a task is completed. Another form of user feedback is to highlight buttons when they are touched, so the user knows that the computer is responding to their selection, as illustrated above.

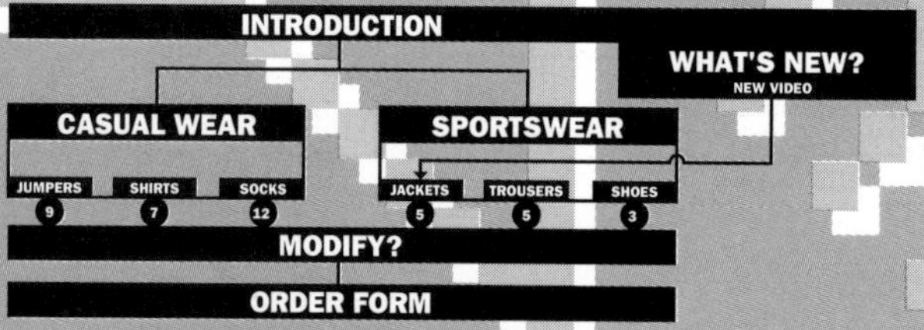

Maps
Maps should be used to provide the user with an overview of the complete data base. They usually provide a graphic representation of all the pages and their relationships to each other and allow the user to move directly to any location in the database, by simply selecting any button on the map.

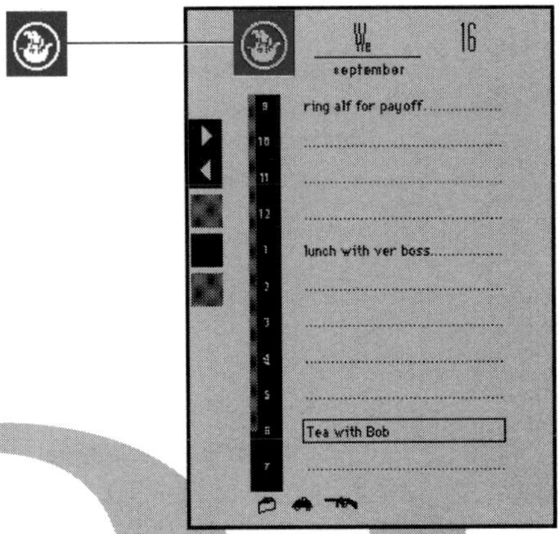

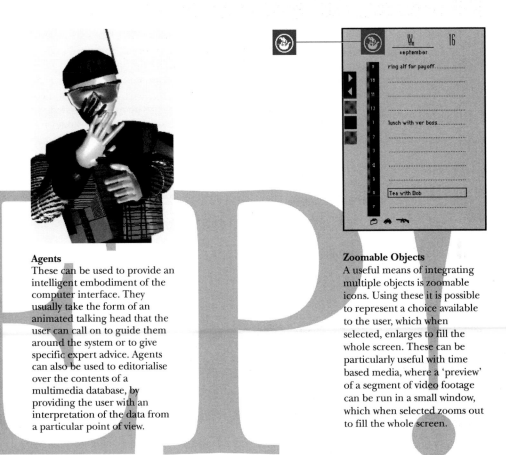

Agents
These can be used to provide an intelligent embodiment of the computer interface. They usually take the form of an animated talking head that the user can call on to guide them around the system or to give specific expert advice. Agents can also be used to editorialise over the contents of a multimedia database, by providing the user with an interpretation of the data from a particular point of view.

Zoomable Objects
A useful means of integrating multiple objects is zoomable icons. Using these it is possible to represent a choice available to the user, which when selected, enlarges to fill the whole screen. These can be particularly useful with time based media, where a 'preview' of a segment of video footage can be run in a small window, which when selected zooms out to fill the whole screen.

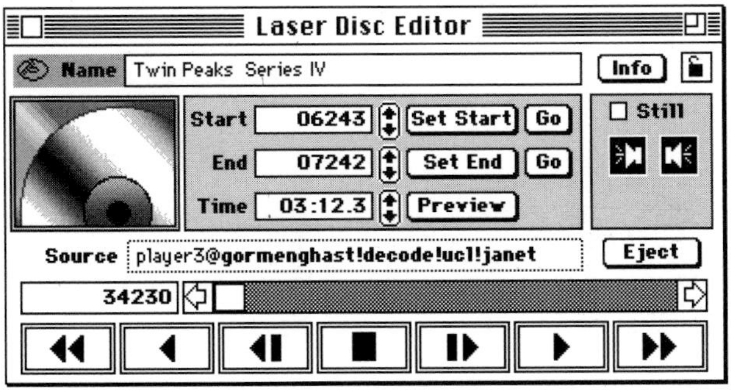

With the integration of time based media, such as sound or animation, into a hypermedia system, it's important to provide the user with an easily understandable control method. The standard metaphor that has been adopted by many designers is a cassette recorder style control panel with play, stop, rewind, and fast forward buttons. Media counters which mirror the counters on most domestic cassette recorders and VCRs are another easy way to provide the user with a means of editing these media types.

DESIGNING a hypermedia product requires a series of discrete stages. In this example we look at the evolution of one screen of a computerised diary, from original conception to working product. In the process of production the diary moved between a graphic designer, an animator and a computer programmer. Each of the people involved in the process makes a critical contribution to how the final product will look and function, emphasising the importance of strong team work in developing hypermedia products.

1 Sketch

Initially it is important to document your concept before you sit down at the computer to begin design work. The original concept should clearly outline the aims of the product along with its key features.

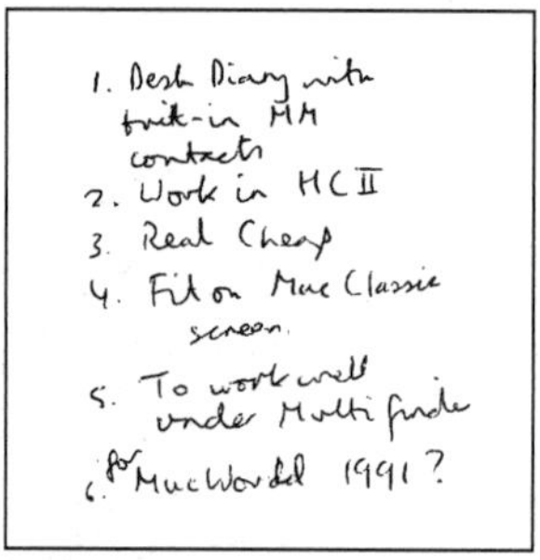

The next stage is to sketch out ideas for the individual screen designs needed. These are particularly useful to visualise how many of the features intended to fit into each screen will actually work without clutter.

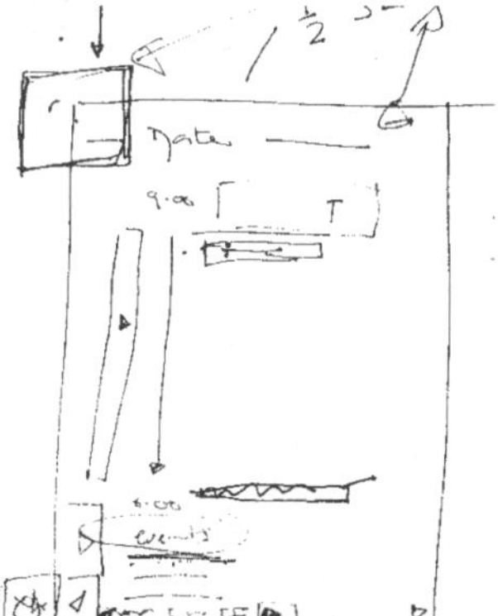

2 Graphics

From the rough sketches you can begin to put together screen designs on the computer. Here it's useful to work in a graphics package to ensure that the focus is on the look of the product, rather than the functionality.

The choice of typefaces used in systems is important to ensure as much information as possible will fit on the screen while maintaining readability. Here the designer elected to create a custom font for the project.

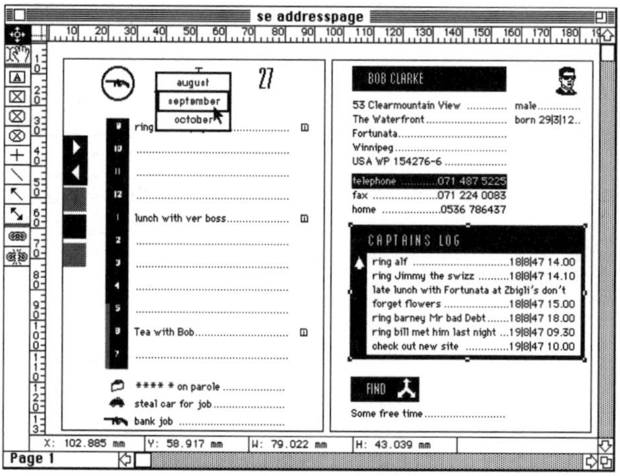

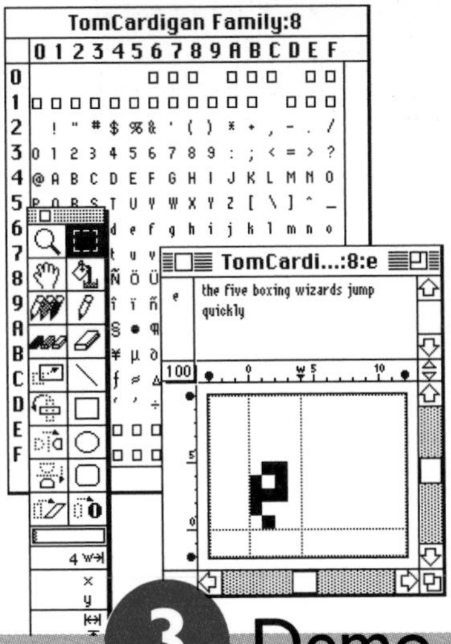

3 Demo

Having completed the screen designs the next stage is to prototype the functionality. In this example an animation package was used to simulate the operation of the diary for the purpose of testing and evaluation. This type of prototype is invaluable in testing the practicality of interactive devices.

4 Script

When all the functions have been decided on, and screen designs approved, a computer programmer is involved to write code to implement the features – and make everything work. A program reaches 'Beta' stage when all the functions have been included, and 'beta testing' is to ensure that everything works.

```
on ChangeAppointment FName Time
  — change existing appointment
  if FName is empty then
    answer newname "Who are you going to meet?"
    if the result is "Cancel" or it is empty then
exit to hyperCard
    put it into FName
  end if
  set cursor to watch
  set cantAbort of this stack to true
  NewAppointment
  repeat
    set cursor to busy
    if the mouseClick then
      WantEscape
      if it is "Yes" then exit repeat — Δ
    end if
    TimeCheck
    if there is a bg field "Day"
    then put it after bg field "Day"
  end repeat
  set cantAbort of this stack to false
end Change Appointment
```

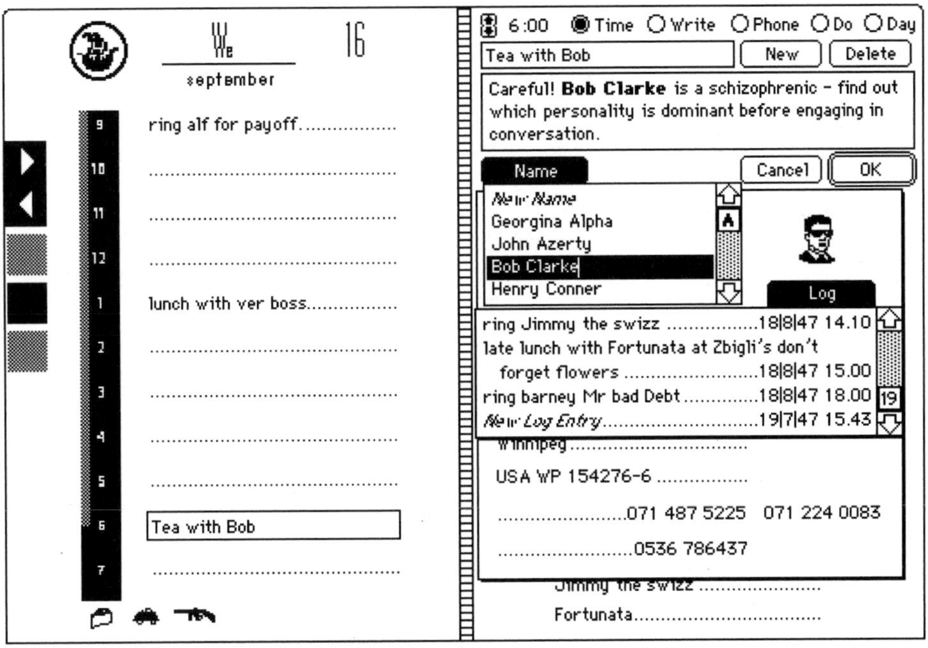

5 Support

Don't forget the manual, user support, free software upgrades, distribution, packaging, advertising, beta testers...

Glossary

Accent symbol which indicates how a letter should be pronounced.

Agent (in hypermedia) video or animated image which gives instructions on using a hypermedia system.

Alignment arranging text or graphics to follow a straight vertical or horizontal line.

Artwork images and text ready for reproduction. Can be direct output from a DTP system (e.g. laserprint) or hard copy and images with manual additions, such as overlays, colour swatches etc. *See also* Marking up.

Ascender portions of lower-case characters that extend above (ascend) the x-height. *See also* X-height.

Baseline invisible line on which letters stand.

Bitmap grid of pixel elements which can be assigned colour values. Also: the method of encoding graphic images in a bitmap. *See also* Pixel.

Bleed illustration which extends beyond the trimmed limit of the page.

Bold type darker, heavier strokes than normal typeface; often used for emphasis.

Brackets used to separate a clause within a sentence or to distinguish parts of a mathematical equation. Rounded brackets are called Parentheses. Use sparingly.

Bullets symbols used to call attention to key points in a body of text. *See also* End-icons.

Cap height the height of the capital letters from the baseline.

Clip art collections of ready-made, copyright free illustrations available in black and white and colour, in book form or in digital form on floppy disk.

Continuation guide guides to reader for navigating symbols through different features usually incorporating arrows or pointers.

Counter the space enclosed within letters like: a, b, d, e, g etc.

Dash punctuation used in pairs to enclose a subsidiary thought used similarly to brackets. *See also* Hyphens.

Descender portions of lower-case characters that extend below the baseline.

Desktop publishing production of finished documents with integrated text and graphics using microcomputer based equipment linked to a laser printer.

Digital font fonts stored electronically which have a simple geometry and are designed to remind readers of computer displays.

Dithering patterns of dots or lines available in some graphics programs which give varying degrees of shading in an image.

Drop caps enlarged initial capital letters indented into text beneath it.

DTP *see* Desktop publishing.

Ellipsis set of three full points indicating an omission.

Em rule unit of measurement of a typeface based on the square of the body of any size of type.

En rule dash in text the width of a lower case n.

End-icons bullets which indicate the end of a section chapter. *See also* Bullets.

Folio page number.

Font design and size of the full range of characters and symbols and the means of printing that design.

Grid non-printed boxes which are used by the designer to ensure consistency between pages of columns of text, positioning of graphics and beginnings of new sections.

Hanging indent the first line left hanging extended to the full measure, while the body of the text is indented.

Hypermedia means of computer access and storage of information which combines video, animation, sound, graphics and text.

Hyphenation instructions for hyphenating words at the end of lines. These should follow rules about where words can be correctly broken up. Will also depend on the justification required.

Hyphens punctuation used to join two words together or to indicate where a word has been broken over two lines. *See also* Dash.

Icons images providing instructions, identifying chapters or introducing warnings e.g. image of a phone to introduce a phone number. *See also* End-icons, Zoomable icons.

Indent space inserted at the beginning of lines.

Justification arrangement of text to give straight vertical edges of text on either or both margins.

Kerning reducing a space between two characters to make them appear closer together.

Laser printer standard proofing printer for DTP.

Leading the spacing between lines of text.

Ligatures two or more letters joined together as a single unit.

Line length length of a line of text measured by the number of characters and word spaces.

Marking up preparation of manuscript for typesetting by specifying typographical instructions or of artwork by giving instructions on colours and special effects.

Metaviews maps indicating to users where they are in a hypermedia system.

Orphans lines of text left over from paragraphs at the bottom of columns; and single words left as the last lines of paragraphs.

Page straps combination of graphics and text which indicate a clear beginning and the extent of a section.

Painting filling in an area of a computer graphics display.

Parentheses punctuation used in pairs to separate clauses. *See also* Brackets.

Perfect binding method of binding a publication by gluing along the actual inside edge of the paper. Used for books and magazines.

Period also called a full stop marks the end of a sentence.

Pixel minute unit that makes up an electronically produced image.

Proof initial or early printing of a document produced so that corrections can be made.

Proofreading the checking of a proof and making amendments or giving instructions using standard proofreading marks.

Range right/left alignment of text at the right or left margin.

Rasterise production of an electronic image of a character using the pattern of pixels which matches it most closely.

Resolution the quality of definition of an image measured in dots per inch on hard copy or in scan lines and pixels on a computer screen.

Reversed out reversal of text or lines from the usual black on white to white on black (or WOB).

Sans serif typeface without serifs.

Scaling slightly distorting characters to fit them in to a given space. Can be used in combination with Tracking. .

Serif stroke which finishes off a letter.

Spiral binding binding by means of spiral plastic or wire inserted through holes in the paper and cover.

Template (in type design) an outline, design of typeface etc which is used as a model for production of text to ensure consistency. Also known as style sheets.

Tracking adding or deleting space between characters to fit them in to a given space. Can be used in combination with Scaling.

Typeface originally the printing surface of a type (hence face) cut into a particular style. In desktop publishing typeface is sometimes used to mean the overall appearance of type.

Widows single lines of text left alone at the tops of columns.

X-height height in a particular typeface of lower-case letters measured from the baseline; excluding the ascenders and descenders.

Zoomable icons (in hypermedia) video image or animation running in a part of the screen which when selected fills the whole screen.